BARBARA'S QUIRKY TALES

BARBARA JONES

Copyright © Joseph Bernard Jones on behalf of the late Barbara Jones,
2013

All rights reserved. No part of this publication may be reproduced, stored in a retrieval system, or transmitted, in any form or by any means, electronic, mechanical, photocopying, recording or otherwise, without the prior permission of both the copyright owners and the publisher. Joseph Bernard Jones has asserted his right to be identified as the author of this work in accordance with the Copyright, Designs and Patents Act 1988.

*

This edition published in Great Britain in 2013 by Farthings Publishing, as a donation in memory of Barbara Jones and in the hope that the MS Society might benefit from royalties for copies sold.

Farthings Publishing
8 Christine House
1 Avenue Victoria
SCARBOROUGH
YO11 2QB
UK

http://www.Farthings-Publishing.com

info@farthings.org.uk

ISBN 978-1-291-48166-2

August 2013 (d)

DEDICATION

This book is devoted to my lovely wife Barbara, always known as Babs, who died on the 16th February 2013. She was very artistic and had a lovely sense of humour that never left her even in the latter years when MS confined her to a wheelchair.

So this little book of her stories is not only to provide you with happy memories of Babs but also to help the MS Society and, one day, I hope, find a cure for this dreadful disease.

Bernard Jones
2013

INTRODUCTION

Barbara's Quirky Tales is essentially a collection of Babs' stories in the Clive and Grinshill Newsletter – I write the Bird Notes for the Newsletter hence her title "Barbara Jones wife of Birdman"!

Babs and I met in Dover, Kent in the coffee bar named Pelosis when I was doing my National Service; she was 16 and I was 19. At the time she pretended to be French and of course I fell for it and only wished I'd done better in French at school! Eventually though when I met her parents I realized that she was not French! Her maiden name was Matsell a name her father brought down from Grimsby. Nevertheless she was born in Royal Tunbridge Wells and was brought up in Folkestone so she was a Maid of Kent. I was born and brought up in Scarborough, North Yorkshire and, strangely enough, I already had a fascination for Kent. When my friend Ted – who later became our Best Man – and I got our first bicycles at the age of ten we began secretly planning a bike trip to Kent (I think then it was more to do with the fruit picking!) Also by chance my Regiment, The West Yorkshire

Regiment, was to amalgamate with the East Yorkshire Regiment and the chosen venue was Dover Barracks by Dover Castle. We were only there 3 months before we went to Aden so it was quite obvious that Babs and my destinies were pre-planned! After I returned from Aden we met up again and married in 1963. We lived in Folkestone, Reigate (Surrey) and York and eventually my job brought us here to Shropshire. In Folkestone Babs worked as a secretary but when we moved to Reigate she managed a music and record department and had many trips to London where she met many pop stars including her then favourite the Rolling Stones! In York she worked for Rowntrees so she made friends across the country most of whom are still in touch. We settled in a cottage (chosen by Babs) in the lovely village of Grinshill in 1976 and, although neither of us had been to Shropshire before we quickly settled in and it became our permanent home.

Sadly Babs developed Multiple Sclerosis (MS), which, oddly, her father also suffered from but her artistic skills and sense of humour never left her. She was quick witted too so when I called her a snivelling southerner her immediate response was to call me a nauseating northerner!!

I think her favourite artistic hobby was creating pictures in needlework and many of her friends have embroidered pictures of their house and garden or their dog or cat created this way.

So we were effectively together for almost 55 years and it would have been our Golden Wedding this year – a long time that has passed so quickly.

Babs died peacefully at home and I was with her to the end. She now rests in peace in the lovely little churchyard of Grinshill Church until I join her one day.

But her humour lives on in her book of her quirky stories so I hope you enjoy reading them.

***

CONTENTS

TITLE	PAGE
Abseiling Grinshill Quarry	7
A bit of a whirlwind	10
A camping holiday in France	12
A pheasant experience	26
America coast-to-coast 1	27
America coast-to-coast 2	29
America coast-to-coast 3	32
America coast-to-coast 4	35
Aunt Daisy and the gasworks	37
Bradley and Barge	38
Every dog has his day	40
Every frog has his day	42
Growing up in the 50's	44
Historic invasions	47
In praise of Mothers	49
In praise of cats	52
Interfering on the home front	53
Lead us not into temptation	55
Life in the 3D	57
Make do and mend	59
My hang-ups	61
My trip to the seaside that never was	63
New kid on the block	65

Phobias, how restricting	66
Regrets, I've had a few	68
Scapegoat holidays	70
Strange encounters at counters	71
Taking the biscuit	73
Things that are dear to us	75
The oriental slit eyed git	77
The Rowntrees reunion	79
The story of Raggy Lugs' lug	81
Thoughts and works of Raggy Lugs 1	82
Thoughts and works of Raggy Lugs 2	85
Tiger, Tiger burning bright	88
The tourist trap	90
What a scorcher	92
White water wobble	94
Z-A letter to the Gas Board	96

Barbara Jones

THREE HUNDRED MILLION YEARS BACKWARDS IN TIME – OR ABSEILING DOWN GRINSHILL QUARRY

Barbara's Quirky Tales

The 5th of July 2006, the day of the abseil, dawned with rain, rain and more rain and we wondered if the event would be cancelled, but no, by the time we'd got ready for Bernard's descent into the quarry the rain had stopped as we waited for our friends Mark and Helen from Shrewsbury to join us. Helen was listed to do the descent and had raised a tidy sponsorship sum from friends and colleagues.

When we arrived at the muddy site already there were quite a few spectators, helpers were arranging shelter and refreshments and a party atmosphere prevailed with sunshine and blue skies – thank goodness!

By now the abseilers were being harnessed up for the descent by RAF PT Instructors from Shawbury. (something Helen was not expecting but I'm sure it pleased the RAF lads!) I must explain that Helen is young and pretty.

Then it was downhill all the way, down the slippery slope of life into the abyss below, led, of course, by our Vicar Rev Rob Haarhoff. Well, what can I say? Fancy being led on the slippery path downhill by the Vicar!!! Well done Rob, we love you.

As we watched the brave participants inching down the quarry, I remember being told of the prehistoric dinosaur, the rhynchosaurus, that once walked here. I think he looked like the drawing but I wasn't around then – honest! So I don't know. Perhaps someone should have dressed up as the monster to welcome everyone as they landed at the bottom…(No, maybe not… this is getting very silly!!)

By mid-morning lots of people had turned up to spectate or abseil and it was great to watch and to socialise with cups of tea and wonderful tasty hamburgers – thanks to Chris for providing these; they were delicious.

Of course, and this should have been mentioned at the start, the reason for this happy occasion is ongoing fund raising for the repair of Grinshill church roof and along with other enjoyable social events we've had, and will continue to have, we'll reach the target.

Barbara Jones

I can't say it yet, at the time of writing, how much money has been raised, but if Bernard's sponsorship is anything to go by I'm sure it will be a wonderful result.

PS: Perhaps by now the results have been published.

Afternote: The abseil raised almost £4000.

***

A BIT OF A WHIRLWIND

How can so many things happen in the space of 5 weeks holiday (sorry, vacation) in Atlanta, USA? Shall I talk about witnessing the robbery, or the shooting, the potential mugging, the terrifying white water canoeing, the swamps - or the tornado?

I'll start with the tornadoes. I mean who else would visit the Deep South in the tornado season? Us, that's who!!

We were leaving a shopping mall late one afternoon and were surprised to find it was pitch dark outside and raining heavily and, because it was dark, we thought we'd stayed too long and Liza (Bernard's sister with whom we were staying) would be worried about us. But it was only 5pm and it didn't usually get dark until 7.30pm. What had happened? We seemed to be the only ones in the 'rush hour' traffic!! Scary or what? Where is everyone? Why is it dark? Are we the only ones left in the world? Are we in a time warp? But wait, no time for vivid imaginations. Do something sensible, turn on the car radio. So we did, only to hear urgent warnings to clear the streets and find a tornado safe area. A serious tornado was heading our way, things were looking bad! But not knowing how to find the 'safe area' we blindly drove back only to find Liza on the doorstep, worried to death and severely reprimanding us for not having tuned in earlier, and had we no idea how dangerous tornadoes can be? Well...no actually!

However, that night we moved the beds into a windowless passageway considered to be a safe area. I recalled reading brass plates in public areas saying 'TORNADO SAFE AREA' Anywhere free of glass, it makes sense.

Barbara Jones

We stayed awake most of the night listening to reports on the progressing tornado but, thankfully, it veered off into the countryside and Atlanta was saved.

The next day dawned fine and sunny, so different from the day before, so we all travelled to Savannah for the weekend where we had a fabulous time in that quaint, old fashioned city by the coast. And guess what? On the way back we were, once more, followed by, you've guessed, another tornado travelling at 50 mph - and the maximum road speed was 55 mph!! I'm sure we exceeded the speed limit on that day! Wouldn't you? Luckily that tornado changed direction too. Thoughts of deja vu crossed my mind.

Life in the fast lane? What will it be next?

Watch this space ...

***

Barbara's Quirky Tales

A CAMPING HOLIDAY IN FRANCE 1971

I recently came across a diary of a camping holiday Bern and I went on in 1971. We lived in York at the time so the first part of the journey was to Dover. We were fortunate though, that my parents lived in Folkestone so we were able to have a comfortable rest before setting off on our adventure.

Friday 20 Aug 71:

The crossing was calm though the weather was rather poor with rain and fog. James Burke was on board – which interested me! We set off from Calais. We were rather tired as we were late to bed the previous night and maybe this was the reason that Bern felt disoriented for several miles before he became used to driving on the right. It rained most of the day but, fortunately, it abated before we made camp for the night. During the day we stopped at a roadside café (equivalent to, say, Fortes) and ordered coffee and salade de saison. This dish took us somewhat by surprise as it turned out to be a lettuce soaked in olive oil and lemon juice at a cost of 2.50 francs! Undoubtedly the most costly lettuce I have ever met! So, lesson number one may be said to be 'be sure you know what you are buying before you spend your brass!'

Barbara Jones

The camp at Dijon was quite good though we remade our acquaintance with the French lavatory that is always rather an unpleasant experience. These however were of the 'modern' flushing type – they flush the lavatory, the floor, the walls and your feet if you have not had the prudence to unlock the door (if there IS a lock) and open it ready for a quick getaway! A constant source of amusement to me is the brush hanging on a piece of string in these 'establishments' to "Keep the lavatory as clean as yours at home"

Saturday 21 Aug 71:
We intended to leave very early in order to arrive at St Tropez before nightfall as we found that we could only average about 35 mph. As it was we left at 10am but in fact this turned out to be a blessing in disguise as we met a family from Herne Bay at a café en route. They had just spent a holiday at St Tropez and recommended us to a camp site at Croix Valmer named Parc Montana and gave us some idea of what to see etc. The beach at Gigaro is, apparently, good and free of charge!

The journey today was more interesting than yesterday and after Grenoble we followed the Route Napoleon that is really beautiful. The road climbs up through mountains and down again into valleys, along gorges and back up through the mountains on narrow, twisting roads with precipitous drops on one side and steep, sometimes overhanging cliffs on the other. It's quite exciting driving! Our mph average dropped to something like 25-30 so we didn't really consider getting to St Tropez before nightfall and, therefore, we decided to stop at Grasse.

Before we arrived we stopped at a roadside vendor (there are many) to buy peaches and a bottle of their local wine. Peaches were cheap, 6 for 2 francs. The wine cost 8 francs, which I thought a little expensive for a 'local' wine. However, it turned out to be delicious. For the record it was a dry white wine.

Barbara's Quirky Tales

On the way we encountered a funeral car. This was rather interesting as it was adorned with black plumes and ornamental 'turrets', something like the old horse drawn funeral coaches. Despite the solemn occasion we couldn't help laughing as it reminded us of Dracula's coach and thought that he had become 'modernised'.

We arrived at Grasse in the dark and stayed the night. Grasse is a beautiful little Mediterranean resort with the smell of perfumes pervading the town. There was a lovely little carving shop – unlike Switzerland the articles are useful things like salt & pepper pots, salad and fruit bowls, egg cups and, of course, tankards! I thought the perfumes were marvellous – which of course they were. I must admit that I really enjoyed walking through the balmy night air with the ever-present scent of a mixture of perfumes in the air. Some of the villas were very beautiful. I particularly liked the roof designs and the chimney stacks with their own miniature tiled roof.

Sunday 22 Aug 71:

Travelled from Grasse to St Tropez. We had our first view of the Med in daylight. The day was hot and sunny. We followed the coast road most of the way and, as it was a winding road my attention was mostly on driving safely. I gave a running commentary interspersed with oohs and aahs on the colour of the sea, the sky, the rocks and the beauty of boats, villas etc, etc. Eventually after almost running down half of the French population (who seem to think that the road is for pedestrians who tolerate cars) cursing in good Anglo-Saxon at hooting motorists, French roads, silly road signs and stupid crossroads – and wondering why the Gendarme blew his whistle so violently- we arrived at Parc Montana only to find the 'Directeur' was engrossed in his Sunday lunch (which appears to be sacred above all things to the Frenchman) and we were informed by the caretaker to come back at 2.30pm by which time the Directeur having consumed, presumably, vast quantities of wine would not turn us away even though his camp site was bulging at the seams! However it turned out that there was plenty of room and we found a lovely site shaded by pine and cork trees. Our neighbours are English – one is an ex-Army Padre and now a Vicar (John and his wife and two young daughters) the other Ricky and Judy and their two young boys. Ricky is in the RAF and is a Lightning pilot! The site is on a hill and below us there is another English couple. He is a Trade Union official. So I said 'Now we have "What a friend we have in Jesus", "Those magnificent men in their flying machines" and "We'll keep the red flag flying" 'to everyone's amusement.'

We visited Cavaliere and looked at the shops. Later in the day, after setting up camp, we went to Gigaro beach for a couple of hours. The sea was fairly rough and we enjoyed leaping around in the waves. We didn't sunbathe today as we considered it unwise on our first day. However, we were reminded of the sun's strength by the odd red patches that appeared on shoulders and collarbones.

Monday 23 Aug 71

Today we visited the famous St Tropez and spent the morning looking at the yachts in the harbour and, of course, the shops. There was little evidence of the much-publicised US Army uniforms in the shops though some of them paid token service to the fad by displaying the odd jungle green tee shirts with some kind of badge sewn on the front. There were however some quite nice clothes though the prices were hysterical! In the afternoon we made our way to Pampelone beach where we had heard it was all happening. It surely was! As we walked onto the beach our first sight was of a topless female calmly walking to the sea. Bern said 'Thank the Lord for Polaroid sun specs cutting out the glare!' As we walked along the beach we saw all kinds of naked bodies but it seemed so natural that it didn't seem at all out of place. We, however, refrained from FFN! The swimming here was superb and we spent an hour or two in and out of the water before hunger drove us back to camp to consume a beef curry with local grown tomatoes. French cuisine hasn't rubbed off on us yet! Tonight we tried an 'expensive' wine – 4f.50! We didn't think it as good as the cheaper wines!

Tuesday 24 Aug 71

This morning we went into Cavaliere. I bought some flip-flops as my sandals haven't lasted the pace and Bern bought a snorkel mask and tube. We then spent 3 hours on the beach where Bern tried out his new toy with much enthusiasm and was delighted. Its great fun to chase the numerous fish and swim for hours with little effort. This will certainly keep him occupied for many an hour!

Later we went to Gigaro again to leap around in the waves. Quite a strong wind was blowing inshore so the waves were quite high.

We returned to camp at 6pm for a meal of lamb and vegetable curry (by kind permission of Mr Heinz!) only to find that Ricky had caught an octopus and was jumping up and down with impatience waiting for Judy to cook it. Our curry, tomatoes and mashed potato seem very trivial now!

This evening we discovered that John is a curate and spent 16 years in the Army as a Chaplain. Another English couple arrived and on introducing ourselves we learned that they were the Allens from Southampton. He is a Trade Union Official (Transport and General Workers). So we now have a Lightning pilot, a Vicar and a Trade Union leader as neighbours. We don't know whether to sing 'Those Magnificent Men in their Flying Machines', 'What a Friend we have in Jesus' or 'Keep the Red Flag Flying'!!

I now expressed a desire to use my Union Jack tea towel as a flag and have a hoisting ceremony each morning with prayers said at the mast. I feel that our trade union friend might raise objections on the grounds that we will be furthering the cause of Imperialism! We feel that any time now he will be coming round to organise shop stewards and gather lists of complaints to present to the Camp Directeur otherwise we will all go on strike and refuse to enjoy ourselves!

Incidentally, each night we have drunk a bottle of the local wine. Oddly enough we have found that the cheap table wines are quite palatable. A wine made at Ramatuelle is only 2f.40 a litre bottle and we like the white in preference to the red or rose.

Wednesday 25 Aug 71

This morning we visited Port Grimaud, a delightful little Venice type town near St. Tropez. The shops were quite delightful. The local bank was advertising a rate of 13f.10 for sterling travellers cheques so I took advantage of cashing £10.00. The equivalent rate in Cavaliere was 12f.60 so I feel justified in congratulating myself on a 'killing' in the world of high finance!!

Bern had a headache this morning, probably the result of too much wine the night before but I administered a soothing dose of Aspirin and guided him to a café to wash them down with 2f worth of Coca Cola! Treatment is expensive in my clinic!!

We then wended our way to Cavaliere beach to do some more snorkelling and sunbathing as our mood took us. After asking a Frenchman the way to the local Post Office (to post postcards to everyone in England!) we were treated to a discourse in French which we punctuated with the odd 'Oui' and 'Merci' though we might just as well have been listening to a Bolivian chatting about the latest revolution! The only thing we understood was his pointing finger – vaguely pointing in a north-easterly direction – and we assumed that the object of our question lay in that quarter. As we left him with many 'Merci's' and 'Au revoir Monsieurs' he continued to direct us until we were out of earshot!

Barbara's Quirky Tales

A word about ants. The varieties are as numerous as the ants! They range from minute creatures to monsters of half an inch! One of the monsters has just attacked me. I must say here that there is one type that has an enormous head (compared to the rest of its body) with huge pinchers. We call these soldier ants. It was one of these that attacked the delicate skin between my toes and Bern had to draw on all the knowledge of his army training to dislodge him! He really hung on with those pinchers but he finally succumbed to a superior force and died a warrior's death. Our casualty is recovering from her wound!

There seems to be a dance on at the bar tonight so we are going over to have a look.

Thursday 26 Aug 71

Last night we went to the camp 'hop' for a couple of hours. They have a very nice little bar there. The music was played disc jockey style consisting of French and English pop tunes. On the whole it was quite good though I thought the French pop music pretty second rate. An unusual feature of this dance was the high proportion of youngsters of age 5 upwards. I thought it rather sweet but Bern thought it unfair to keep kiddies up until 11.30 at night. However, it was quite good fun.

It rained this morning! I was quite upset about it. The rain soon stopped but it remained cloudy all day so I spent part of the morning doing some much needed washing whilst Bern had an interesting chat with Ricky about cars and flying! Later we visited Grassin, a tiny village on the top of a hill nearby. During the afternoon we went into St. Tropez to gaze at the yachts and the sea and to buy some fish. Unfortunately, fish is sold only in the mornings so we had to make do with tinned fish from the supermarket! We later feasted on fish (which incidentally was delicious) peas, tomatoes and the inevitable mashed potatoes.

Barbara Jones

After dinner John and Barbara invited us over for a noggin and a chat. They are very interesting people and seem to know someone in every town and hamlet in the country!

We had a walk round the site and discovered that it is enormous. Amazingly we ended our walk at the shop so seizing the opportunity we purchased another bottle of wine and took it back to the tent to slurp in the moonlight. The Allens paid us a visit (they had moved further up the hill to a caravan this morning) and they told us about another beach just by Cavaliere harbour and about a market that is held there each Wednesday. We will no doubt visit the market next week!

We've booked a meal at a nearby restaurant named La Bergerie for tomorrow night at 8pm. As it is Bern's birthday I've condescended to take him out for a meal – at great expense of course! We are really looking forward to our first French meal.

Friday 27 Aug 71
Happy Birthday Bern!!

Went into Cavalaire this morning and did some shopping then swimming and snorkelling in the afternoon. We returned at 5ish to get showered etc ready for our evening out. Our meal was at 8 o'clock so we dolled ourselves up a bit. I wore my long skirt and a lovely crocheted top.

La Bergerie is quite a pleasant little restaurant situated on the edge of a vineyard and is built of stone with wooden beams inside. The lighting is dim but all the tables have candles giving the place a warm, romantic atmosphere.

For the first course I chose Charcuterie Variété, which is various cold meats, for example salami ham and garlic sausage served with black olives and a crinkly leafed lettuce. Bern had Oeuf Mayonnaise. For the main course we both chose Entrecote avec des Herbes with Frites. I had Petit Pois and Spaghetti L'Italienne and Bern had Haricots

Barbara's Quirky Tales

Vertes; for the sweet I had Glace Café and Bern had Crème Caramel. The whole meal was quite enjoyable though Bern said he would have preferred his steak without Des Herbes! The wine we chose was a relatively expensive Rose (7f a bottle!), which however was delicious.

All in all it was an enjoyable meal and we had quite a laugh at how they cooked the steaks. Every so often a huge flame shot up in the kitchen to a height of at least 3 feet and this as far as we could gather was the way to cook a steak. I must say that the steak was rather rare - but blackened on the outside!

Finally I admitted defeat and left a little of the vegetable and spaghetti but Bern finished his off in the usual hoggish manner!

We ended a very pleasant evening with beer and coffee and left at 11.30pm. No hurrying you away from your table here! This is one of the most enjoyable parts of French eating. There is no hurry and no waiter hanging around to grab your empty plate and push the next course under your nose. The French may be a bit earthy in some of their habits but they are very civilised eaters.

Incidentally, John and his family departed today after many 'goodbyes'. They got to know nearly everyone on the site so they had quite a send off!

Saturday 28 Aug 71

Decided to go into Port Grimaud and change the remaining travellers cheques then went to Pampelone beach. We had arranged to see Ricky and Judy there but we were unable to find them. Having found a suitable place we got down to some swimming and sunbathing – I tried out a bit of topless which I rather enjoyed!

We came back for a meal of Cannelloni with chips from the camp chip shop and tomatoes then we went into St Tropez to see the night life. The naked bodies were now covered with an amazing variety of fashionable clothes each person trying to out fashion the others! There were mini dresses, long dresses, hot pants, long pants and, the ultimate surely, see-through hot pants!!

There were entertainers galore from hippy guitarists to clowns. One interesting chap was a fire eater and demonstrated his skill by eating balls of flaming cotton wool with the comment 'Bon Appetit' from a British lad in the audience. He also amused everyone by taking a mouthful of paraffin and blowing it at a flaming torch creating fireballs.

On the big yachts other 'clowns' were entertaining the masses by eating their dinner on the deck with all the pomp and splendour of our Imperial past. Mostly the boats were registered in Panama (to avoid certain taxes?) but it was obvious that they were American or European owned. One even had a large gold Buddha squatting in the middle of the table for heaven knows what purpose – unless it was the posh pepper pot!

Sunday 29 Aug 71

We decided to go a little further afield today and so we made our way to Cavaliere sur Mer. It turned out to be a delightful little bay and we spent some time swimming. The water was fairly shallow for some way out and it was quite warm. Bern found a rocky headland to explore and snorkelled happily for an hour or two among the rocks and underwater 'canyons'. Great fun!

On the way back we came across a lovely little sheltered bay at Le Rayol. Here we took a few photos.

Arriving back in Cavalaire Bern bought me a cassis ice cream as it is my favourite and Bern had one too. They really are delicious. Bern says I aptly described it as Ribena ice cream!

In the evening Rick and Judy invited us in to crack a bottle of wine with them. Later Rick and Bern sneaked off for a beer at the bar much to the annoyance of we girls and much to their school boyish prank delight!

Barbara's Quirky Tales

Monday 30 Aug 71

We awoke later than usual this morning due no doubt to the late hours of the night before. I wasn't grumpy, as I <u>didn't</u> have a hangover!

We all went down to Pampelone beach around midday. Rick has a boat there so he and Bern took off for some snorkelling at the headland across the bay while we girls threw away our inhibitions on the beach.

Bern said the snorkelling was great fun as the water was very deep and the rocks numerous. Alas they didn't see many fish nor did they sight the object of their search an octopus. However, they snorkelled merrily for one and a half hours and finally returned to the boat with a rock fish – a rather dangerous type with poisonous spines on its top fin! The 20-minute boat ride back to the beach was great fun as the sea had become choppy. At one point they missed a rock by inches and had a retrospective fright when they imagined what it could have done to the little boat. At last they arrived at the beach, wet through, cold and a bit fatigued to be confronted by the girls displaying nature unadorned! Unabashed we opened a bottle of wine and drank to 'bosom friends'!!

As the sky was beginning to cloud over we all set off for St Tropez to see the sights – the girls to see the shops and Rick and Bern to fortify the wine with a drop of the local beer at the Café de Paris!

And so we returned to camp, hungry and a little merry, to consume vast quantities of chips, sausages and the inevitable tomatoes. Later Bern and I went over to the bar to round off the day. There was a film showing at the hastily erected open-air cinema. It was 'One Million BC'. Out of curiosity we had a quick look over the canvas 'wall' and saw a diplodocus roaring in French!!

Tuesday 31 Aug 71

This is market day in St Tropez and as I'm drawn to market like bees to a jam pot we made our way there to see the local wares. It was quite interesting but the prices put us off somewhat.

Incidentally we found a mouse in our food box this morning. He was a charming little fellow even though he had consumed half a packet of mash potato powder! The local fauna cause us great amusement what with an army of ants crossing near the tent, a gecko in the tent one morning, a tree creeper, large grasshoppers and now a mouse we are thinking of starting a zoo!

This afternoon we spent on Cavalaire beach sunning ourselves and swimming and snorkelling then we returned for a meal of tinned meat, chips, peas and carrots. No tomatoes today!!

In the evening we visited Grimaud a charming little village situated on a hill surmounted by a castle that is floodlit at night. Quite a strong wind was blowing and in the dark, narrow streets it seemed quite spooky. We came across an old church with slit windows and as I shone my torch through the window we saw a face seemingly staring back at us. It turned out to be Mary the Virgin – there are not many left in these parts!

Tomorrow is our last day so we are going to make the most of it. In the evening we hope to have a farewell 'party' with Rick and Judy. Just think we can all get smashed on, say, 4 bottles of wine costing 8 francs, which is about 60p!! Fantastic!!

Wednesday 1 Sep 71

On our last day we decided to have a look at all the places we'd got to know so well. So we visited St Tropez, Pampelone Beach (for my last 'naughty' sunbathe), Gigaro and Cavalaire. Bern went mad and bought me a cassis ice cream and gave me some francs to spend on a present for myself! I bought a pottery ashtray! It has a handle with a hole strategically placed to enable it to be hung on the wall. I rather think it won't be used as an ashtray!!

Barbara's Quirky Tales

We returned to feast on Cannelloni, mixed vegetables and the inevitable frites, then we took a couple of bottles of wine round to Rick's caravan for a farewell party.

Thursday 2 Sep 71

We struck camp and set off for Grenoble. The journey through the mountains was marvellous the Gorge de Verdun being particularly notable. It's about 1000 ft deep and the road wends its way round the top of the gorge giving fantastic views and exciting driving! It really is beautiful.

Alas, the mountain roads were too much for the car and before we arrived at Grenoble we heard an ominous crack from the rear of the car then a scraping noise and we realised that a spring had broken. We limped on, stopping from time to time to do what I can only describe as what we could and at last reached Port D'Ain at 11pm!

Here we camped the night deciding to rise early and seek a garage to fit a new spring.

Friday 3 Sep 71

Rose early as planned and set off for Macon where there is a BMC garage (the car was an Austin A70). At last we arrived, nerves in tatters and one of the tyres in shreds through scraping on the bodywork. The garage, as usual, couldn't help and advised us to go back to Lyon. We thought that this might be a wasted journey because if they didn't stock the part we would have lost 100 miles so we decided to press on. At this point Bern hit on the idea of tying up the axle with the tow rope and 'hey presto' it worked although we had to stop every 50 or so miles to jack up the car, take off the wheel, pull the axle forward, re-tie the rope, replace the wheel and carry on. Eventually, however, he managed to tie down the broken spring and tie the axle tight enough to prevent it moving back and thus keep the tyre clear of the bodywork. It now held and we limped into St Gobain at 10pm tired and dirty but pleased that we had been able to get so far. We only had 150 miles left and, with luck, we should make it alright.

We visited Bernard and Danielle and met Pascal who was staying with them. After chatting for a couple of hours Bernard kindly took us to his mother's house to stay for the night. The bed was very welcome as we were shattered.

Saturday 4 Sep 71

We woke early and found ourselves in a French house. It was very nice apart from the usual toilet troubles that seem to plague the French. An unusual feature of the washroom and toilet was the frosted glass door on each. We couldn't decide why but came eventually to the conclusion that the people were 'kinky'!!

At 8 o'clock we went with Paul to Danielle's house for breakfast. This was rather unusual too as coffee was served in what I can only describe as soup bowls! The menu was bread and butter, croissants and biscuits which we timidly approached until we saw our hosts dipping bread or croissants into the bowls of coffee and munching happily. We followed suit. When in France...(to adopt a phrase)

The coffee was finally slurped by raising the bowl in both hands much the same as the Chinese do. To round off this unusual breakfast we had a glass of liqueur (in this case crème de cassis). We were assured that this was quite normal!

Having said our goodbyes we set off on the final nerve racking stage of our journey. The car behaved very well and we arrived in Calais at 2pm. We decide to have a meal as we had missed the chance in Dijon. At last we tried escargots (snails) and found them delicious- not unlike winkles but not salty.

And so we boarded the ferry to Dover............

***

Barbara's Quirky Tales

A PHEASANT EXPERIENCE
(or close encounters of the feathered kind!)

Recently a vision wondrous to behold appeared in our garden and it's true to say that our lives and those of our neighbours have been enriched by Gustav Klimt our resident pheasant. I call him Gustav Klimt because his richly patterned plumage reminds me of Klimt's famous painting ' The Kiss' of two lovers wrapped romantically together in a sumptuously patterned long cloak.

This stunning bird has all the natural attributes in his colourful markings of the decadent cloak that Klimt was attempting and succeeding to portray on canvas.

Gustav visits us, and everyone else, for breakfast, then returns for lunch, and, if we are very lucky, afternoon tea. We rarely see him after that. Perhaps birds don't need evening meals. Maybe we don't either, but that's a subject best avoided so I won't attempt to go there! Let's just say we could learn a lot from the habits of others.

When Gustav first arrived he came with his Missus, equally beautiful but less colourful. Sadly, we found her dead in a heap nearby on the road, the result of someone driving too fast I should think. Poor Gustav mourned with heart wrenching noises, so distressing to hear. But now the noises have ceased and maybe, in time, he'll find another Missus we hope.

Before I go I must bring Gustav down to earth when I say he walks with the cocky head-butting jerk of Uncle Albert in Only Fools and Horses! Sorry Gustav, but you do. Then, of course, there's the tail.

What a tale...

Barbara Jones

AMERICA: COAST to COAST - PART 1

Bernard and I have recently had one of our Big Holidays, something we don't often have these days, so its all the more precious when we do.

We flew to Atlanta to stay a few days with Liza, Bernard's sister, in order to attend her son Christopher's graduation from the University of Georgia in Athens. Athens, north of Atlanta, is a lovely, 'olde worlde' university town, old by American standards, with lots of shady trees and old, elegant Georgian buildings. Its all very gracious and pretty, very establishment and orderly. Family values and old money come to mind.

The ceremony was held in a huge football stadium and the graduates, approximately 2300 of them, all filed in and sat on chairs on the pitch in their various academic groups, all in their caps and gowns, and to the accompaniment of very stirring classical music played through the sound system. The stadium was soon filled with families and friends and, with 2300 or so students, you can imagine how many people there were. It just had to be held in a stadium.

There were speeches from professors, including the head, and other academics, and the very first black man to attend the university, who is now a well-known professor also famous for other things. Well done for forging the way.

Then the degrees were announced and each group stood up accordingly to great applause, turning their mortarboard tassels from right to left to signify their new status before throwing their hats in the air! All so different from over here. They didn't, as we do, go up individually and shake hands, as it would have taken far too long. So many beautiful men and women graduates all enjoying themselves. All that and brains too... not to mention hard work!

After the ceremony the exit was all very well organised, it would have had to be and it was. We were impressed. We drove back to Atlanta and, in the evening, we all went out to a restaurant to celebrate.

The next day Bernard and I flew to San Francisco for our exploration of the west coast and Yosemite, and the Grand, Bryce, and Zion Canyons. Two and a half weeks later we flew back to Atlanta and then visited Charleston in South Carolina. It's a toss-up which is my favourite, San Francisco or Charleston.

So next time I'll be boring you silly with part two of the holiday.

Can't wait? !!!!

***

Barbara Jones

AMERICA: COAST TO COAST - PART 2

...and then...after the graduation we flew from Atlanta to San Francisco, from temperatures of 90F in the east to 68F in the west and I wondered why all the women on the flight were carrying jackets! I wasn't carrying one of course and my only cardigan was in the suitcase. What did you expect!

After collecting the hire car we drove through the city to the hotel, unpacked the precious cardigan and made our way to Fisherman's Wharf where we sat in a restaurant overlooking the Golden Gate Bridge over there - Wow! Alcatraz over there, sun setting over Oakland Hills in between and, behind us, Pacific Heights - Wow! Below us was a huge colony of sealions all squabbling noisily and all piled on top of each other on large, wooden rafts. There must have been over 30 rafts, all heaving with wet sealions of all sizes (a huge, unexpected tourist attraction) and what a noise they made; not to mention the fishy smell.

Barbara's Quirky Tales

Next day we learned that it was easier to explore San Francisco by bus than by car so this we did and saw all the sights aboard a very efficient network of well run buses.

But the best thing just had to be the helicopter flight over the city the following day. Stunning views and no fog. The pilot, a big, handsome ex-firefighter (drool! drool!) picked me up and lifted me on board when the step up proved difficult!! Yes, really!! The highlight of the holiday - and the flight wasn't bad either!!

Seriously though as well as a perfect flight he flew us <u>under</u> as well as over the Golden Gate Bridge. What an experience to see the city from the air.

After another night we collected the car and travelled to Yosemite National Park. Wow! yet again. The Tioga Pass had only just re-opened after winter snows - and this was now May and still plenty of deep snow piles around. Stunning mountain scenery, fabulous waterfalls falling over 2000 feet, weather warm, cardigan back in suitcase!.

Then came the 'big drive' 560 miles in one day to the Grand Canyon, passing through Death Valley on the way in early morning before temperatures rise to over 140F by the afternoon. Impressive. Next, but not stopping, Las Vegas. I know its different at night but lets keep going!

The chain of Best Western hotels we stayed in were excellent but the Grand Canyon hotel was one of the best and, when we arrived, four elderly male hippies, all on their Harley Davidsons were gathered outside. Bless their hearts, all wearing their bandanas, earrings, neckerchiefs, leather waistcoats and walrus moustaches, all over 60 and from Pennsylvania. Having spent the summer of '59 on the back of a Harley I was intrigued. They were delighted to pose for photos but insisted that I pose with them and, being an old hippie myself, I was delighted.

The Grand Canyon - what can I say but Wow! again but it will have to be next time as time and space are running out. If you can bear with me, there won't be bears

Barbara Jones

unfortunately but more canyons, the drive back through Las Vegas - equally impressive?! California coast, lovely towns, the Big Sur and sweet little sea otters. Then back to Atlanta and the Charleston visit.

So here's to the next time - I know you can't wait !!

***

AMERICA: COAST TO COAST - PART 3

Here we go again flying over the Grand Canyon, this time in a 12 seater aeroplane, the only way to realise just how vast and spectacular it is. At first glance, as we stood in awe, it occurred to me just what the early settlers must have thought when, after trundling along in their horse drawn covered wagons over quite flat scenery, suddenly coming across the most spectacular barrier of all time. What were they to do? Find another way I suppose and, being brave pioneers that's what they did, although someone might have remarked "I say chaps these new world natives have gone a bit deep with the plough don't you think!"

After that we travelled on to Bryce Canyon, all pink stone and carved into weird, twisted shapes like stalagmites in a vast cave but this is outdoors. You drive to vantage points along the way to look down and up at cathedral shapes, twisted castles and arches - in fact anything you want them to be. Spectacular to say the least, in changing colours and shades of light.

Barbara Jones

After a two night stay in a lakeside hotel we set off for Zion (our last canyon) in a heavy snowstorm but when we reached Zion three hours later the snow had gone and a hot sun was shining, surreal to match the scenery. Zion is smaller and you drive through the valley floor and look up at the jagged mountains, quite different and less wild. Our hotel, which had a balcony, was built of logs! "So what?" I hear you say, except that all the furniture, including the huge bed, was also built of logs - but not the mattress thank goodness which was amazingly comfortable!

Having been 'canyoned out' as it were, it was back to the California coast, attractive seaside towns and miles of vineyards (including one called Bernardus!) and the impressive, rugged Big Sur coast. Everywhere is spacious and unpopulated. Towns such as Monterey and Carmel are well worth visiting. Clint Eastwood is no longer the Mayor of Carmel but Doris Day walks her dogs on the beach. Sadly, we didn't see either of them. Were we really expecting to? No, of course not but it would have 'made our day' as it were if we had. We did, however, see stunning artworks displayed in art galleries, super shops, fascinating houses - no shortage of money here.

One of the many quaint seaside towns we visited reminded me of the gold rush. All wooden buildings and lots of bars and restaurants and there it was, a huge emporium beside the beach full of furniture and all sorts of things. We entered California's answer to Stretton Antique Market, full of the same sort of bric a brac - or clutter as Bernard calls it! It was very interesting and I fell in love with a glass table lamp which would have presented problems of how to get it home (it wasn't worth the price of shipment) and it would have needed rewiring. Bern's answer to the problem was quite straightforward - we just forget about it! A man's answer to everything I think!!

Oh, I forgot to mention the sea otters. There they were in abundance, swimming up and down on their backs cracking seaweed pods on their fat little bellies and stroking their whiskers. A joy to behold.

All too soon it was San Francisco again and back to Atlanta and the visit to Charleston which deserves an article on its own.

This is becoming 'The Forsyte Saga'. So stop yawning and I'll write more next time!

***

Barbara Jones

AMERICA: COAST TO COAST - PART 4

And so it was, upon returning to Atlanta from San Francisco that we, along with Bern's sister Liza and her grown up son Chris revisited Charleston in South Carolina, a long car journey taking all day. Mostly the town was how we remembered it from the 1980's only perhaps a little more prosperous with a huge, beautiful new suspension bridge over the river Cooper. The rivers Cooper and Ashley flow each side of Charleston before running into the sea. The most desirable part of the peninsula that it forms is where all the antebellum mansions look out to sea. One can spend ages exploring all the old streets and gazing in awe at the wonderful architecture and those with a sea view are the most spectacular. All houses have verdant, semi-tropical gardens and the perfume from the magnolias was a bonus for us - even if the hot, humid sun was not!! But plenty of shade was available from all that lush vegetation.

All the lovely old shops and the large indoor market were very tempting, mostly selling tasteful, arty crafty things. There was no tacky tat - I don't think the locals would allow it!! We wanted to buy Liza a surprise present but what would she like? I have a theory...we observe her

Barbara's Quirky Tales

reaction to all the goodies and the loudest "WOW" wins!! The loudest "WOW" was for a large framed print of a fox. It out-wowed the Audubon heron print that I would have bought, which proves you can never buy someone a picture unless you know it's the one they want. She was delighted with her gift.

We stayed at the Marriot Hotel, all very posh. Liza had previously booked a very good deal on the internet. The hotel was undergoing refurbishment and the rooms would be finished but there would be scaffolding up and decorating etc. going on so the rooms would be $60 a night. On arrival we found there to be no scaffolding, just a very pristine looking hotel. Liza, with sinking heart, approached the desk clerk thinking the deal would be off but, no, she had booked the deal in good faith and so it stood. The refurbishment had been completed ahead of time and Chris, being very aware of a bargain, noticed the tariff on his bedroom door which now said $300 a night.

A good deal? Well done Liza!

Before leaving Charleston we visited a nearby mansion with fabulous grounds full of wildlife. We saw some outdoor former slaves' huts and each was big enough for 2 rooms, a large bed, a fireplace in each room and somewhere to wash. I can think of hovels in this country where working people were less well off. Comparatively, those that worked in the mansions and grounds were well fed and treated better than others I think; having said that all this slavery, of course, should never have happened.

After a very enjoyable visit we returned to Atlanta where we spent a few more days relaxing in Liza's lovely house and swimming pool. We dined out at the equally lovely houses of her friends who treated us to legendary Southern hospitality.

Ah well, back to Manchester - RAIN !!

***

Barbara Jones

AUNTY DAISY & THE GASWORKS

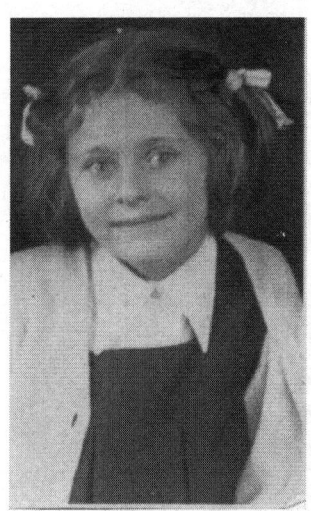

When I was eight years old, Great Maiden Aunt Daisy came to stay with us in Folkestone, where I was brought up, and it was down to me to show her the sights of this once grand Edwardian seaside town. The sea, the stately cliff-top walks, the posh shops etc.

But no, I thought she would much prefer to see something far more exciting. You see I'd discovered where the Devil lived - and it was the gasworks. A sight wonderful to behold. There was a huge mountain of coal at one side of the road being shunted across a bridge where it descended into a fiery furnace of blazing cauldrons from hell. I was convinced that the Devil was stoking the fires. After all, wasn't that what we'd learned at Sunday School?

We arrived, and I waited and waited for a glimpse of horns and tail while a very confused Aunty Daisy waited for an explanation. She was not impressed when a sooty looking workman asked if we were lost!

Later that, day as we sat in a teashop, Aunty Daisy said Mum and Dad would play hell with me if she told them.

I replied that if we went back to the gasworks then the Devil could play hell for real!

Poor Aunty Daisy, what an awful child.

***

BRADLEY AND BARGE...TO THE TUNE OF BONNIE AND CLYDE

Hello and big 'Woofs'. SHE can't think of anything to write so I've stepped into the void – once more into the breach dear friends. So here I am again, the world's most handsome golden retriever, well that's what I think and who's to argue? Well Barge might; he's the young pretender from across the road, a pale coloured retriever much younger than me, a mere juvenile. We go walkies together whenever his owner is away. With my superior knowledge and experience I can teach him how to find the latest rabbit holes, squirrels, other dogs and, best of all, how to chase cats. Not that he needs my help as these things come naturally to us. We also play 'hiding from the owner'. We love watching the frustration on their faces when they call us and we pretend not to hear!

By the way, Barge is not his real name, he's really called Monty but he comes over here barging into everything with so much youthful enthusiasm that SHE says he may as well be called Barge because he's built like one anyway!

Of course afternoon 'walkies' is at 3pm. It's a social event among the humans. A small gang of them go but these days only Barge (when he's with us) Pickles and Mouse and I seem to be the only dogs. Very sad because at one time there were more of us.

I've had to lecture Barge on what happens when we encounter coffee tables due to my experience at my master's previous place of work. I mean, really, who would have them at that height? Only silly humans when they are entertaining, that's who! You see we have very strong, very thick, very beautiful tails that automatically wag when we greet people. We can't help it when hot coffee or tea, sugar, milk, cake and biscuits all collide and afternoon tea all comes together. We try to mop up the cakes and biscuits but for some reason that is just not acceptable! The only people who love us are the carpet makers – it's a sure thing no one else does!!

Oh, did I tell you Barge loves to cuddle whereas I don't see the point. I love everyone but can't take part in vulgar demonstrations. Besides, I get too hot. But he leans all his weight on anyone who kisses that noble dome shaped head. SHE needless to say wishes I could be like that.

Goodbye for now. Look forward to shaking paws at a future date.

***

EVERY DOG HAS HIS DAY

Hello, or rather – woof. I'm Bradley and I'm having MY say. About time too I hear you utter after all these 8 years. SHE sat there wondering what to write about so I said "What about ME, am I not worth it?" Really it should be obvious that if all these famous ladies on the tele think they're worth it then why not ME? I've learned by now that if you don't think you're worth it then nobody else will. That's MY opinion coming from a huge, handsome Golden Retriever with a pedigree to be proud of which is more than SHE can say! Anyway she wrote a previous article about a silly cat called Deadly Dudley that they had years ago in York and I felt rather miffed at so its my turn now.

My birthday is on the 11th September and I was one year old on that terrible never to be forgotten day in New York. Took the shine off I can tell you but I know I could have helped all the other sniffer dogs doing valuable work if only I'd have been there.

Barbara Jones

I'm very lucky really; my master is retired and I have at least 2 or 3 walks a day and it keeps him fit too (not to mention walkies in the car!). He walks with other humans and their dogs. My best friend is Millie, a King Charles spaniel and gundog like me. Can't say too much or Daisy, my other girlfriend also a Golden Retriever, may get jealous! I know she wants to marry me. A case of Daisy, Daisy give me your answer do. SHE, my mistress, (her indoors) keeps singing that to me. How predictable, how boring!! My master says she's very silly and I agree. We males must stick together at all times.

Then there's Roxy, an Airedale who comes to see us. She's very snooty and elegant and sits on the chairs. Why can't I sit on the chairs? That's because I moult and she doesn't. Oh well, at least my combings out (such gorgeous fur) goes to carpet bird's nests, a good cause, birds have such good taste! Then there's Chuffer; he's one of the boys but I don't see him quite so often and my old mate Max has left the area so I don't see him anymore.

In the evenings I go for a quick drink down the pub. I'm very popular with everyone and cheesy bics and crisps are gratefully received. But sometimes we go posh and go up to the Inn and I'm on my best behaviour as usual. Everybody loves me and I'm in with the in crowd – or should I say Inn crowd! One-upmanship SHE calls it.

On my master's birthday in August we had a barbecue and party. All this glorious food for me. I don't have to beg - so demeaning – I just sit in front of everyone and look neglected so they can't resist me. I'm not silly I just come between them and the food that's all.

By the way, I dislocated my tail. The Vet realigned it and said that Labradors and Retrievers often do it because they wag too hard. It still hurts a bit and I'm being brave. Perhaps its payback time for wagging coffee pots, milk jugs cups and sugar off tables in the past. Oh I did so enjoy it but its odd that no one else did! Humans are funny creatures aren't they??!!

Barbara's Quirky Tales

EVERY FROG HAS HIS DAY

Anyone who has a pond will know what happens in Spring. Frogs arrive en masse for the annual get-together and oh! what an orgy, or rather what a frorgy, they were having in our pond. It's only a small pond but we counted over forty of them all having a wonderful time. And the waterfall, affectionately known as Viagra Falls, certainly lived up to its name!

The frogs, having accomplished what they set out to do, have now all deserted us leaving the eleven goldfish in peace. Loads of frogspawn was left, some of which I think the fish have feasted on. The fish haven't been exactly virtuous either. After ten little ones were purchased last year one vanished, cat's dinner perhaps, and another one died. There's not enough room for the heron to come down so he can't be blamed. It was naive to think they wouldn't multiply and we now have eleven; maybe there's more now the frogs have set a good example! I hope some of the old frogs and some soon to be new frogs return to the pond and live there as they have before. Its wonderful to hear them croaking softly as you sit quietly and listen. All I ask is you remain lovable frogs and not turn into handsome young princes as you are supposed to do. What an awful thought. Please stay as you are.

Which reminds me of the sweet little fairytale of the young princess who lost her golden ball in the Palace pond. As she stood crying a frog appeared and frightened her. "Go away, I hate frogs" she cried.

"Well", said the frog, "That may be true but I can rescue your golden ball. Think how cross your Daddy will be when he realizes you've lost his valuable birthday present." Knowing she would be in trouble she agreed to the rescue. But the frog said only if he could come back and live with her in the Palace and sleep at the foot of her bed. She reluctantly agreed. He kept his distance and all was well.

But one night as she slept froggie hopped up and and sat by her face admiring her beauty. It was all too much for him, he gave in and kissed her lips. At that moment he turned into a handsome prince and, do you know, to this day her mother still does not believe it!!

Well, would you???

***

Barbara's Quirky Tales

GROWING UP IN THE 50'S

We were discussing, my friend Annie and I, how life was for us in the 1950's when she suggested I write about it. Seeing as how nothing had materialised in my mind for this article, here goes...

One thing that really sticks in my mind is coming home from school on Monday afternoons to be greeted by the strong smell of soap suds and the damp washing hanging up to dry in the kitchen if it was wet outside and it usually was. The humidity and the smell of soap would be almost overpowering as we sat amongst it all to eat the dinner of cold meat left over from Sunday roast and salad or veg depending on the time of year. The following day we'd have the rest of the meat minced up in Shepherds' Pie or Cottage Pie. We did have a mincer that would screw to the end of the table and mince the meat. Very posh!

Bedtime was memorable because of dreading to brave the cold by going upstairs with a hot water bottle to a cold bedroom. Few people had central heating then. We'd all sit around a coal fire, scorching at the front and freezing from a draught at the back. I don't think insulation had been thought of then! I suppose most houses then were rented and landlords didn't care – I know ours didn't. I remember women with mottled legs caused by sitting too close to the fire something you don't see now thank God. Also in those days hardly any woman wore trousers

We didn't have a TV then and didn't have until 1959 so Mum would usually sit and sew, Dad would read the newspaper. I would read a book or do homework all to the accompaniment of the radio. We did have something called conversation and discussions and even storytelling. All people seem to do now is watch television – or so it seems.

On to house décor; nowadays its big business, everyone wants to make a mark on their own home but then it wasn't like that. Most people couldn't afford to decorate their own houses let alone buy them. There was lots of brown paint making everything seem dark, everyone had lino and rugs and it was a bonus if you had lovely antique furniture because the new furniture was so awful. Due to the war everything was basic as there was little money. People could leave their doors open, there was no fear of being robbed. What would be the point? Everyone had the same things; no one had anything worth stealing. Does anyone remember the three flying ducks on the wall? Everyone seemed to have them. Luckily Dad painted lovely water coloured pictures of old houses and quaint views so we had lots to fill the walls with. He also did pictures for other people and I would accompany him to Rochfords, an Artist's shop in Folkestone, on Saturday afternoons to have the pictures framed. I can still remember the smell of oil paint, the wood, the linseed oil and seeing all the other paintings just like an art gallery.

I think in these austere times we needed some escapism so we all went to the pictures at least once a week. We would watch things like how the sun-bronzed Californians lived it up on the beautiful beaches in the sunshine with their fast cars and then we would wait in the cold wind and rain for the half past ten bus home.

Then it all seemed to change in the late fifties. Mary Quant and her Ginger Group dresses came along and we had something to call our own. We didn't have to look like our mothers. Instead of looking like a child one minute, then leaving school and resembling clones of our mothers the next, like having to wear hats and gloves, we suddenly had clothes of our own. They were expensive but well worth saving for.

Things got even better after that. The 1960's came along, financial circumstances improved, we started going abroad and Terrance Conran's Habitat opened up giving us spaghetti jars, wine carafes, beautiful furniture, in fact all the wonderful things we'd been craving for. We were all a lot better off and dreams were coming true. We got married in 1963, bought our own new house, filled it with Habitat furniture, discovered Provence, wore fashionable clothes and lived the dream. I wish the 1950's could have been the same.

***

Barbara Jones

HISTORIC INVASIONS: WE SHOULD HAVE BEEN THERE - BUT PERHAPS NOT

Hello and Happy New Year. Hope you had a festive Christmas. We, like everyone else had an extremely cold one snowed in on the Yorkshire coast at Scarborough not able to visit York or Whitby but we enjoyed a good family time indoors – much too icy to venture out.

As I sat in the warm indoors surveying the view of a very cold, grey North Sea I imagined I could see Viking ships approaching from savage, cold northern lands - I'd obviously had too much to drink!! But no, wait, this is perhaps where Bernard's ancestors would have come from and I think that by now, Bernard, it's time to remove that hard helmet with horns as we've come a long way since then. You've only got to watch a local rugby match to know this isn't so. Keep it on Bern it suits you!!!!?

I could just imagine as the Viking long ships came menacingly near the leader, probably Sven or Thor, they usually are, stood up and said " Now lads when we land I want you to set fire to the towns, kill all the men and rape all the women – and don't get it wrong this time!!"

Being married to a Yorkshireman of maybe Viking descent I can truthfully say that what you see is what you get. At least you know where you stand with no frills attached. Very honest. For example, you could spend all day cooking an exotic meal and he'll say " Aye lass that were a good bit of roughage." And if you were to wear a gas mask, as you do, he'd say, "You look nice dear." But if you were wearing something new he would instantly notice and want to know the price so you'd start ripping off buttons while saying "What, this old thing?" But then we all do this don't we? Don't we?

Barbara's Quirky Tales

Perhaps I'm descended from the Norman invasion. Oh I do hope so! I would have enjoyed the charming Gallic approach but I think, in fact I know, it would not have meant a thing. Oh well, vive la difference for what its worth. We often tease each other about our differences. I point out his ruined Scarborough castle and brown, crumbly cliffs and compare our intact Dover castle and stunning white cliffs although Scarborough wins as a seaside resort even if the climate is a little too bracing!

You see he is a nauseating northerner and I'm a snivelling southerner so we live in the midlands and compromise. I only hope you all understand and kindly bear with us!!

***

Barbara Jones

IN PRAISE OF MOTHERS

Hello! I've just realised Mother's Day is 3rd April and this seems an appropriate time to write about my mother who sadly is no longer with us and Mother's Day doesn't mean much when you can't indulge your own mother.

Raggy Lugs is on strike. He says he's done his bit for now and he's left this article up to me. He never knew my Mum he arrived after she departed but I'm sure there would have been massive cuddles on both sides except that he doesn't cuddle but she did. She loved our two previous golden retrievers.

Mum could be a rather vague character sometimes who would completely put her trust into the male population and let them look after her. That's because she had to look after Dad for many years until he died and she did it so well. No one could have done it better. She also had the gift of managing money perfectly.

When I was growing up Mum could be very strict but also fair. But she also had a childlike quality that was very endearing and made you want to protect her but she could flip the coin instantly and become very dictatorial and sensible.

I always remember her showing me things by example. Every Sunday huge busloads of children from London's East End would travel down to Folkestone where we lived so they could play on the beach and romp in the sea as all children love to. Of course snotty little snob me would make a fuss and say how dare they play on our beach and use all the facilities. How common. Mum heard this and the very next Saturday she hauled me onto the London train and took me to the East End and the Docks to show me all the devastation the war had caused and in 1947 there were still huge bomb sites and slums you couldn't believe if you tried and kids with hardly any shoes all playing on the bomb sites. Mum opened my eyes as to how lucky I was to live in comparative luxury right by the sea and to not have to suffer sea sickness enduring a hellish 72 miles on a double-decker bus. Now I think about it I can't imagine how anyone could endure that. I felt differently about London children's invasion after that.

Mum also took a shine to Betty my school friend. We were six years old and she would invite Betty to tea to play with my dolls once a week because Betty had nothing and Mum thought I should learn how to share things.

On Mum's last visit to us we arrived back here after picking her up from Folkestone to find a mouse had ransacked the sideboard in his quest for the dried sunflower seeds and things had fallen on the floor. At the time I was proud of my display of sunflowers. I was tired of Mum's constant talking and being tired I blew my top! All she said was that some people arrive home to find they've been burgled; you've had a mouse. Big deal! I'll never forget that.

***

IN PRAISE OF CATS
DEADLY DUDLEY THE TERRIBLE TABBY

Deadly Dudley was a huge, beautiful grey and black tabby cat, a real battle-scarred, war torn bruiser with holly-leaf ears and a thick ringed tail. It was easy to mistake him for a wildcat - and people did!

He was a voracious hunter and would stalk anything that moved. He would bring his prey home and let other cats through the cat flap to share his bounty. I suppose he thought that if we had parties then so should he! We made a cat flap operational one way only - he could get out but not back in. So he would sit outside and meow pitifully until George, our then next-door neighbour opened the flap for him.

Being a real mean moggy he loved to chase dogs! No dog was safe in neighbourhood - even big dogs were threatened. Having been to Crufts a wicked thought occurred to me. Why not smuggle him in!! Of course I never dared but can you imagine the headlines

"Chaos at Crufts, Cat Wreaks Havoc! Pedigree Dogs Flee in Terror!" I'm sure the dogs would have had a ball.

We no longer have cats, just one big dog who...guess what? Yes, he chases cats. So the roles are at last reversed. I must point out though, that Deadly Dudley cannot be blamed for the decline in the Clive/Grinshill bird population as all this happened a long time ago in York.

Barbara Jones

INTERFERING ON THE HOME FRONT

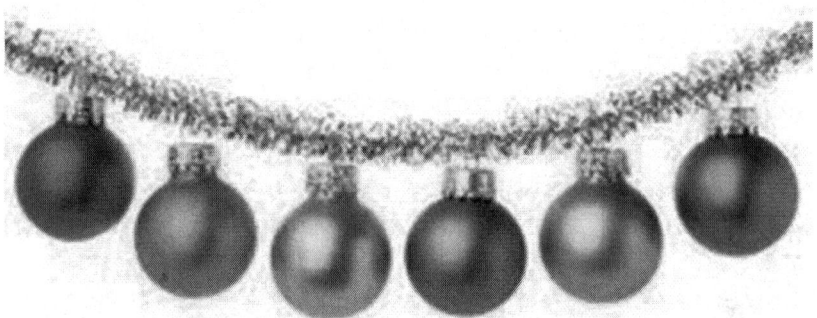

Once upon a time – or was it twice? There was a frustrated wannabe interior designer desperate to be let loose on a poor, unsuspecting public. Yes, it was me, and thankfully for everyone it never happened, although sometimes my advice <u>has</u> been sought due to massive interference on my part. I just love planning where to place things and in what settings those things should be.

This time of year it gets dark early and oh what bliss! People light their houses and draw the blinds much later so someone like me can have a sneak preview as we drive past. No, its not noseyness – honest – its more about wanting to help and advise people on how to maximise space and light, not to mention what the décor should be, but I wouldn't dream of doing this because everyone's ideas are different and most people would feel like maximising <u>my</u> space for interfering!!

Folks these days don't need help due to all the wonderful TV programmes we see. I can't get enough of them, but in contradiction, if the very dishy L.L. Bowen wanted to change my room I would say 'no'. I have other ideas for him!! And as for Phil and Kirsty and their Relocations it is very true. To me location is everything; perhaps its why we live in Grinshill. I'd rather live in a small abode with stunning views than in a mansion on the moors. Bleak or what? I love it when Kirsty wants to knock down walls and Phil tells her what would happen if she did. Those two should be married to each other!

But back to me!! If money and talent were plentiful I would love to redesign and decorate houses, first consulting with the client, then moving in with my team of workers to make the dream come true. I would supervise and then collect the cheque when the work was finished. But in reality I know its not as easy as it looks and I admire the effort and hard work it takes.

Bernard wonders if all this is the sign of a misspent youth and yes actually he's quite right. As a child I had sometimes to be prised away from my playmates to go with my mother to visit an old great aunt and to talk, yet again, about the war! To a child too young to remember it was very boring. So, having been told to sit and read, I would, in my mind, redecorate her house from top to bottom and refurnish it with added rocking horse of course.

So – yes you could say it's a sign of misspent youth!!!

***

Barbara Jones

LEAD US NOT INTO TEMPTATION

This time I won't bore you further with the American holiday. The memories have kept us going all winter. But hey! Spring is here with thoughts of how to look good for the new season. At the start of every winter I dream of going into hibernation huddled down amongst a heap of grizzly bears (itchy but warm!) and we all sleep through the dark and bitter cold to emerge, thin and sylphlike and flyaway to flaunt our new selves in the spring sunshine and summer fashions. Oh Ha! Ha! Ha! Dream on Jonesy...at the moment wearing a burka would be more appropriate.

Every year I fool myself into thinking a miracle will happen and by Easter I shall look like Twiggy but the effort has to come from me. Of course we all know what and what not to eat including the one about eating all you like but don't swallow it (a trick to be avoided at weddings and dinner parties). We try to obey the rules and we're doing just fine but then, through no fault of our own, an advert comes on the television telling us "This is no ordinary food, this is M & S food" and we watch, mesmerized, as the wonderful food is heaped onto the fork and we succumb to temptation. Just when things can't get any worse along comes Easter and all those choccy eggs and hot cross buns. Why? What have we done to deserve it? Christmas was bad enough! (If you must buy me something for Easter then perfume will do nicely thank you – you can't eat that!)

But I had an idea so I've put it into practice and, sometimes, only sometimes, perhaps rarely, it works...

Oh, alright then it hardly ever works! You fancy chocolate so you pretend to unwrap a favourite bar and you sniff it, break it up and slowly savour it remembering every detail of how it tastes, you roll it round your mouth, chew, swallow. This takes all of 3 minutes, the time it takes to eat a real one. Afterwards, you are supposed to feel satisfied – well that's the theory anyway. But when you return to reality and realize it was all a dream you feel even better. Mind over matter. Naturally it works better after a big meal, but try it and, if it works for you, I'll treat you to a Kit Kat!!

***

Barbara Jones

LIFE IN THE 3D DOWNSIZING, DAYDREAMING AND DEVON

Downsizing – no not us, simply because we've never had to upsize although a third bedroom would be nice. What we have here has always been right for us and the rooms are not poky. You may wonder why I'm saying all this; it's just that I'm trying to justify our house with one in Devon we've seen – or should I say I'VE seen! Enough said!!!

I don't think people realize just what downsizing means because when we sold our 2 bedroom terraced cottage in Bishopthorpe, York it was advertised as just that even though it had a large front and back garden. A middle-aged couple came to view and, seeing a door under the stairs, assumed it was down into a basement and large cellar. The lady asked how many attics we had. Oh excuse me, if that was the case it would have been advertised as such. Then to top it all she said they'd never fit in all their furniture.

I was by then deeply curious to know where they were moving from only to learn they lived in an enormous four storey Victorian terrace in Leeds. They weren't looking for a holiday let either. I could have understood that, but no, they wanted somewhere to retire to. After that we sold quite quickly through an estate agent to someone more realistic.

It's like saying that perhaps the Loch Ness monster might like to downsize to Ellesmere Lake! Now that's a thought; think of the tourists it would attract!

Back to real life. We've just returned from a week in South Devon having explored everything in the most glorious weather, the fabulous scenery, all the mind blowing river estuaries, towns, landscapes etc. I saw a small house for sale on a hill overlooking the Teignmouth estuary. The house frontage faces a busy road (calling for double or triple glazing!) but the southwest facing back overlooks this glorious, wide estuary with all the little boats bobbing up and down at high tide and lots of birds at low tide. I said LOTS OF BIRDS BERNARD!!!!!!

The words forget all about it come to mind when all the practical bits were pointed out – down to earth with a bang. Needless to say having driven past a few times en route to our hotel there was no interest in viewing!! So we don't know the price, the parking situation, the back garden, the state of the interior – nothing (although the outside looked pretty good).

Purely 'Dreamtime' as the Aborigines would say. I expect by now the place has been sold for a lot of money, perhaps as a holiday property. Now there's a thought, but even so we couldn't possibly afford a magnificent view like that. As I look out at the view we <u>do</u> have its pretty special and if the Estate were to flood the fields between here and Hadnall we'd have a big lake with boats wouldn't we? It would be a compromise but daydreams cost nothing do they??

***

Barbara Jones

MAKE DO AND MEND – LIKE WOT I DO!

Happy New Year everyone. It's never too late to wish folks that and this is my first opportunity. Let's hope the recession doesn't bite too hard and we all do as well as we can until the 'promised' recovery happens. So we just have to sit it out and make the most of what we have – we've been there before and survived. Which reminds me, I've just spent a fortune on dry cleaning having examined clothes that I've kept for years because they are too good to give away or throw away. And why would that be? Because they are of good quality material, well made and didn't cost an arm and a leg in the first place.

So I'm now updating them into the 21st century and, as I don't tend to follow the crowd, it doesn't really matter about the style as long as they're imaginative and not too way out. That's not to say I won't buy new things to wear with them. A lot of money can be spent on accessories can't it??! Not to mention the odd good purchase from a Charity shop (or Dress Agency if you're feeling posh!) I've had some wonderful designer clothes in the past, being of the mind that something second hand of good quality takes priority over something new that falls to bits after three 'wearings'. As we speak I'm sitting here pulling what's called pilling off a new sweater, which is very attractive. Charm it has in spades but sadly not quality.

Before Christmas I saw an advert for something you can buy from Pound Stretcher for de-pilling knitwear. Santa didn't bring me one so I will buy one but it won't be used on the clothes that have stood the test of time.

In a throwaway society I don't pretend to understand the Economy and the small amount spent on a de-pillar won't restore it but I will not spend good money buying poor quality goods that fall to bits just to keep everyone in

Barbara's Quirky Tales

business because if everyone in business upped the quality then maybe things would be different.

Talking of Christmas I hope you all had a good one. We enjoyed it but not the extremely cold weather – but it <u>is</u> seasonal after all. Whatever happened to global warming? I'd been wearing so many layers to keep warm I thought maybe I needed to use a bookmark to know how far I'd got because it took so long to undress for bed!!

Perhaps after reading this I'll be guaranteed a place on 'Grumpy Old Women' – I'd really love that.

***

Barbara Jones

MY HANGUPS

The other day while sorting out the wardrobe I thought to myself, 'What if our clothes could talk to us?' After all, in their own way they all have personalities. I expect mine would say 'Ouch, you've stretched me too far' , 'I'm much too good for you', 'You're too old for me' or 'You're not posh enough and not what I had in mind as I hung in the shop'.

But, much worse, what would they say to each other? Imagine the competition amongst them to go places or even go anywhere at all!

My work clothes suffered the worst, same place every day, even though they were expensive.

And what about the holiday selection? So nerve wracking for them, not knowing for sure right up to the last moment who's going. You've passed the test, you've been selected, only to spend the holiday still in the suitcase and not see wonderful places. And all the catty bitchiness. For example, 'I'll scratch your hooks and eyes out if you go out to dinner and I don't!'

Every so often there's great excitement and anticipation over a wedding or Summer Ball. Everyone's on tenterhooks (or even coat hangers!) awaiting the outcome. Then, hush, the door opens and a glamourous new arrival makes its entrance and everyone knows the outcome! Oh the jealousy, the tears, the tantrums, the unzipping of emotions!

Worst of all is the relegation to Charity shop or jumble sale. But then, maybe, just maybe, every jacket has a silver lining and someone will give my clothes a better life and love them, tatters and all. They deserve it!

Of course mens clothes don't have that problem. Most of them are happy to snooze away in the shirt drawer and not go anywhere at all and, if this article convinces you I'm totally round the bend - then you're quite right. ------> Blame the heat!!!

***

Barbara Jones

MY TRIP TO THE SEASIDE - THAT NEVER WAS

by Raggy Lugs the world's most handsome retriever

Hello! Remember me? She's dug me out of hibernation to write this because she can't be bothered! I was so looking forward to my seaside visit, but, guess what, I was left en route with friends in Surrey. I was not invited to the 70th birthday bash at the very posh Leas Cliff Hall in Folkestone, which, according to them, was wonderful as was the posh hotel they stayed in opposite the venue. Me and my bad manners would certainly not have been welcome there even though I try not to sneak into kitchens or slurp from my water bowl. Sleeping on the bed might have been a good idea though. Now I'll never know how comfortable it was or how good the food was will I? But their friend Yvonne, whose birthday bash it was, loves me and knows me very well because she comes up here to stay with us and I'm sure would have invited me if she could.

What really upset me was their graphic description of how rough the sea was. I was so looking forward to galloping along the beach at full speed with the wind in my fur and the spray in my face. Apparently the weather was fine and sunny if a little cold and windy which suits me fine. Pause if you will just to imagine what it was like for them and what it was like for me to miss it!!

Our friends Bill and Gwen in Horley, Surrey who often stay with us up here made me very welcome and fed me well but it happened to be Guy Fawkes weekend and if he wasn't dead he certainly would be if I could get my teeth into him!!! It started with a big public display followed by lots of children's back garden festivities and the noise was horrendous. I have to admit I was terrified, a big brave dog like me! I got between my hosts on the sofa and, according to them, couldn't stop shaking. They drew the heavy curtains, turned the television on full blast and cuddled me but I could still hear all the loud, thunderous bangs and whooshings.

Perhaps that's what air raids were like in the war. So, please, just think of us frightened animals and keep us safely indoors. We don't want to spoil your fun but please try to limit it to one night only with a minimum amount of bangers. Surely pretty fireworks that don't make a noise would be preferable and more pleasing to the eye. What do I know? I'm only a helpless, dependent animal but I do have a voice and I want to be heard. Woof, Woof!!!

Excuse all the whinging and moaning. To make up for it I was treated to lots of walks in the woods and hills of Surrey so I can't really complain – but I do, so there!!!!

***

Barbara Jones

NEW KID ON THE BLOCK

Exciting news, we have a new arrival of the canine variety in Grinshill. He is the sweetest, nicest puppy you've ever seen; a mixture of Yorkshire terrier, Jack Russell and Shih Tzu and his name is Bertie. He belongs to our friend Annie who's very proud of him. Everyone he encounters falls in love with him. Who wouldn't? He is tiny and mostly black and grey with a very raggy, tousled, shaggy coat. The ears are now standing up but folding over at the top in unruly, most enchanting tufts of fur. He also has long whiskery tufts round his nose and chin and I think he looks like a very dishevelled Denis the Menace. Maybe he's descended from Denis the Menace!!

He's at the moment very tiny but getting bigger and stronger every day. We notice it because we see him most days when Annie and Bernard and sometimes others too go on the 3pm dog walk ending up in our conservatory where we have a cuppa and play run and fetch Raggy Lugs' toys. That's when we notice that Bertie is getting bigger and stronger and can now squeak the squeaky toys instead of just carrying them around.

Raggy Lugs is very tolerant of the new arrival not seeming to mind when the huge tail is swung on and used for transport! He also doesn't mind Bertie jumping up to kiss him. That's quite a long way to jump. We notice the difference in size- a good example of 'Little and Large'. I can imagine Raggy Lugs thinking 'Oh dear will he grow bigger than me? I hope not but when he's older I can impart my superior knowledge and we can go hunting or ratting behind the tool shed together but for now we wait patiently for nature to take effect'.

I think at the moment Bertie most resembles the Yorkie in him, that's why he gets on so well with Bernard!!

***

PHOBIAS, HOW RESTRICTING CAN THEY BE?

Ugh! My only phobia snakes. I've always had it – can't even look at pictures of them. It's not their fault; after all they are Gods creatures and beautifully marked as well. They have their uses too. I can remember reading about the annual Texas rattlesnake roundup where the people kill as many snakes as they can and there are prizes for the biggest skins. And now, guess what, Texas is overrun with rats! No prizes for guessing who eats rats. Why, the snakes of course. Serves the people right. So perhaps I'm on the snake's side after all!!

In theory nothing would be greater than to trek through the Amazon jungle. I'd love to but for one thing. Imagine coming face to face with a twenty-foot long anaconda. I don't think so.

Spiders and other creepy crawlies I love but others don't and many have phobias about spiders. I often see them scuttling round the warm coving in the lounge but I don't mention it to friends or they'll all get up and go! So phobias are funny things and we have to work hard to control them. I remember pointing out a particularly huge spider to a lady at work only to cause such fear and panic I was quite sure she was going to die. So I stopped doing that. I also stopped going to the pet shop where Simon, the owner, always showed me the two pythons whereupon I would make a quick exit!

On another occasion we were in the Okefenokee area of South Georgia, USA just north of the Everglades – not my choice of venue I must admit but Bern, me and his sister Liza were bird watching at the side of a quiet country road and I was standing next to a large, black, worn out car tyre when, suddenly, this 'car tyre' uncoiled itself and all –

must have been twenty feet of it – slithered off into the undergrowth. When I'd recovered Liza told me black King snakes are harmless and that people keep them in their gardens to ward off poisonous snakes. Well that's okay – just don't go into people's gardens even when invited!!

There are other snaky tales but this one is at my expense. I'd bought a very nice silky python printed dress which was fine on me and on the hanger. I took it home and tried it on again but when I unzipped it the dress fell around my ankles and there was this huge python wrapped around me. I needed to step out of it but I was frozen on the spot with fear and couldn't move. So I had to wait until the fear subsided before I could escape. Needless to say I returned the dress. So feel free to laugh, I did when I'd recovered my composure.

How silly is that?? Answers on a postcard please – but no, perhaps not!

***

Barbara's Quirky Tales

REGRETS...I'VE HAD A FEW...BUT THEN AGAIN...

I expect we've all done things we regret or not done things we should have. In this case it was in Morocco – well where else would it be?!!!

A few years ago we went on a week's break split between Marrakech and Essaouira and on the first night on these city breaks everyone gathers in the hotel foyer to meet everyone else before having dinner in the restaurant. On a table set for one a lovely, smartly dressed, dapper, elderly gentleman sat trying to look cool and at ease with being on his own. We wondered if he would prefer company so we invited him to join us. Never has anyone moved more quickly as he brought his cutlery and bottle of wine to our table. We shared a lot of wine and on hearing where we were from it transpired that he had spent the war stationed at RAF Shawbury and he knew just about anything and everything that happened around here including first hand knowledge of many pubs including The Elephant and Castle here in Grinshill and lots of places in Shrewsbury. He proved to be very interesting and entertaining. Since the war he had lived in lots of places had married and was now, sadly, widowed but had one son now a successful business man in Australia of whom he was very proud and two lovely daughters who lived near his home. He loved his frequent visits to Australia to see his son and grandchildren. Home to him now was a flat by the sea in Bournemouth.

So after a most interesting evening we ate with him every night and also enjoyed trips out together until it was time for us to travel to Essaouira and for our friend to fly back home. I remember a hurried goodbye because the hotel transport that would take us to the coast was early and the taxi to the airport hadn't yet turned up. Not the easiest of times. Very stressful.

On our way to Essaouira we passed surprisingly green fields full of not cows but baby camels and goats standing on the top of wide argon nut trees eating the nuts. They are obviously not allowed to eat them all – very surreal indeed.

In the confusion of leaving Marrakech I remembered our friend and hoped he'd got to the airport in time and I realized with sinking heart we hadn't exchanged addresses or 'phone numbers and now we never would. All we knew was that he was called Jim and lived in Bournemouth. I had wanted to invite him up here to stay with us and visit all his old haunts. I'm sure he would have loved it. It would have brought back many memories for him. Perhaps he was hoping we would invite him. That's why I've always felt bad about it and often thought of trying to trace him but realise by now it could be too late. Its not as though the journey here would have been difficult because he mentioned he always had a taxi door to door when I asked how he would get home from Gatwick Airport.

How could I have been so thoughtless? I should have asked him as we sat over our leisurely evening meals.

I wonder if he still remembers us?

***

SCAPEGOAT HOLIDAYS

The scapegoat, by William Holman Hunt 1854-6

Whilst on holiday getting blamed for everything, as we women do – for example it rains – my fault, the car won't start – my fault, the hotel is too noisy – my fault I'm sure it all rings a bell! However I suddenly had an idea. Why not capitalize on always getting the blame, make some money for another holiday and get blamed again!

I reckon most couples have big arguments on holiday so why not spare blaming your wife, take me with you (all expenses paid of course) and then blame me for everything instead thus ensuring you and your wife have a perfect holiday!!

Mind you I don't come cheap and somewhere warm and exotic will do. I'll keep a low profile and only pop up to get blamed. On return expect to get an extra bill for humiliation!

So, having launched Scapegoat Holidays dot com etc response has been very slow – I wonder why? One can only assume that most couples enjoy having a good row with each other, no third party involved, as part of an enjoyable holiday!

Oh well, seemed like a good idea at the time. Must go, I'm off to Barbados – don't ask!!

***

Barbara Jones

STRANGE ENCOUNTERS AT COUNTERS

Whilst in town the other day I overheard an old lady say to a shop assistant, "He does it when he can but he doesn't when he can't".

It sounded so funny, the mind boggles as to what she was talking about! We can only wonder – and it's best if we leave that one alone don't you think? Perhaps it was the gardening!

But it made me think of the unexpected things people say to each other, not to mention conversations between complete strangers and what we overhear in passing.

When I lived in York I travelled to work by bus from one side of the city to the other and, about halfway there, a lady of about my age would get on and sit beside me if possible and get off in town while I continued to work. We would talk about everything under the sun but rarely about each other. We never even knew where each lived or worked, our lives, our marital status even our names – nothing. But despite that we were very close. Then one day, just before we came to Grinshill, she said, "you know when getting old some people get ever so, ever so fat and some get ever so, ever so thin don't they?" I was wondering what was to follow when she said, "I'll get ever so, ever so fat and you'll get ever so, ever so thin". And with that she got off at the bus stop and I never saw her again. Very strange. But I wish I could see her again now all these years later to tell her how wrong she was because I'm the one who's going to get ever so fat and she is probably ever so, ever so thin!

But stranger than that was the encounter my Mother and I had when a well dressed, distinguished looking, elderly gentleman in a Department Store. I was about 4 years old and carrying my beloved, moth eaten teddy bear from whom I wouldn't, for anything, be parted. You couldn't get new teddies then so he was second hand. His head had been sewn back on twice. He looked like Frankenstein's monster and he only had one eye but it mattered not to me. I loved him. The elderly gentleman was passing the time of day with my Mother when he paused and said, "Is this your daughter?" Mum said, "Yes". And then he said "And is that her teddy bear?" Mum replied that it was. He stopped and looked at us for a while then said to my Mother "She'll probably marry a very ugly man". He doffed his hat and walked off. We never saw him again. Well I think he was wrong on that one – but maybe it's all a matter of opinion!!!

Answers on a postcard please –but no, perhaps not!!!!

***

Barbara Jones

TAKING THE BISCUIT

Before he retired Bernard worked for the MoD for many years and during that time he visited a lot of MoD locations in different parts of the country and, whenever possible, if I could, and if it didn't interfere with my work I would accompany him and we would sometimes stay overnight in the Officer's Mess which we both enjoyed. The food was always good and I can honestly say we were well looked after.

One of our favourite venues was Longtown in Cumbria; a cosy place with stunning scenery but it is now closed down due to Government cuts.

We were able to take Bertie our previous golden retriever and he loved it. Everyone made a fuss of him and he dined like a lord thanks to the generous kitchen staff! But the icing on the cake for him was being let loose in the extensive grounds to chase huge brown bunnies all day (and night if you'd let him!). He never caught any but it kept him busy. I've never seen rabbits quite that big or so many.

One particular visit there sticks in my mind. It was a few years ago just before Christmas. The weather was good, the journey pleasant and as usual as we got near Bertie, sensing, perhaps smelling his beloved bunnies, would become restless and very excited. We would open the car door; he would be gone and not seen again for hours. Meanwhile we would check into the Mess and have a drink.

At Christmas the staff would always go to great pains to make the place look magnificent with masses of floral decorations, lots of baubles and fairy lights, huge real log fires and, most of all, two enormous floor to ceiling Christmas trees equally decorated with all sorts of lovely glittering things, wooden toys, tinsel, shiny balls in all colours, candles, more lights, stars, fairies, and lots of heart shaped ginger biscuits tied up with satin bows; very Scandinavian. Everything was perfect – or so we thought.

I'll leave you to guess!!!

So we sat by the firelight glow in the truly wonderful Christmas atmosphere as we perused the tempting dinner menu. Bertie rushed in, you'd think he'd have been exhausted after all that bunny chasing but no, he seemed alert as he sniffed the air. Could this be a clue as to what happened next? We, in this magical mood had no idea. Can anyone guess?

After a few minutes Bertie moved from the fireside and disappeared while we continued to bask in the warmth. Suddenly there was a loud crunching noise followed by a gentle swaying of one of the Christmas trees followed by more crunching noises and things falling to the ground.

Have you guessed yet?

Then we saw Bertie reaching up into the tree and pulling down, yes, you've guessed, more heart shaped biscuits – he just had to demolish them all but not before he'd re-arranged the rest of the tree. We managed to redecorate it with the help of the staff who thought it was extremely funny but I don't think the Army shared that view. I wonder why???

Footnote from Raggy Lugs: -He wishes you all a Merry Christmas and so do I. He says he wishes he could have done all the things Bertie did but then he has Bernard's full attention and lots of walkies whereas Bertie had to be left while we went to work; I was part time. So maybe Raggy Lugs is better off than Bertie was but I do think in fact I'm sure that Raggy Lugs, presented with the above scenario would have done exactly the same thing. I'm sure you agree.

*****

Barbara Jones

THINGS THAT ARE DEAR TO US
The Purple Apothecary Jar - Everyone should have one.

On passing a furniture shop back in 1962, I noticed, displayed on a teak sideboard a large, glass apothecary jar. Instinctively I knew I had to have it but was told by the salesman that it was a display item and not for sale. I pleaded with him and finally bought it for £25 – a huge sum in those days.

I then had to tell a puzzled and very irate fiancé that it would look wonderful on <u>our</u> teak sideboard (very fashionable then), that, at the time, we couldn't afford to buy!

Cart before horse comes to mind!!

Eventually, furniture was purchased and my pride and joy took centre stage on the new teak sideboard in our new marital home. My new husband, now calm and resigned, had to admit that it looked good. But it's funny how instincts pay off. All these years later the sideboard has long gone but the purple apothecary jar still shines on.

A good buy?

Goodbye.

***

Barbara Jones

THE ORIENTAL SLIT EYED GIT

Not the greatest of compliments to pay a very beautiful chocolate point Siamese cat is it? Well he came to us as a kitten from Norfolk – not the mysterious Far East as he would have preferred and having said goodbye to Deadly Dudley our big butch war torn but oh so cuddly British tabby I was less than amused when Bernard walked in with what can only be described as a small, skinny, cream coloured ferret! That's what they look like as kittens before the brown points start to come.

I called him Chang Chang and tried to bond with him but I couldn't, even offering to give him to Bern's Mum (who liked Siamese cats) if after a week things didn't work. In the end I felt sorry for this helpless little soul who would sit round my neck or on my lap, not because he loved me but because he was always cold. He would wrap himself up in the corners of bedspreads and sit under table lamps in the hope that the lamp would warm him. The worst moment was when he sat too near the fire and set his tail ablaze! Having snuffed his tail out I realised how cold and helpless he was.

I blame the Army Officers for having discovered them in Thailand, then known as Siam, and brought them back to England whereupon most of them died and only the hardy ones survived the cold and were then bred to become a hardier breed but why didn't their coats become thicker? Their British cousins have thicker coats to cope with the weather but these poor things haven't evolved one yet. Why couldn't the British Army leave things alone? I suppose if they had we'd never have known these lovely cats.

As Chang Chang grew up he became a very beautiful cat you couldn't help but love, but so intelligent and inscrutable. Oh for the uncomplicated British moggy who knows his place! I felt that Chang knew he was smarter than me – I didn't much like it! He would always be one step ahead when you played with him as if in a game of chess! He also became selectively destructive. We had some long, loosely woven curtains that became his rope ladders and the whole house came to resemble an assault course in his pursuit of the odd fly. But, and this is weird, being inscrutable he would sit and look at me intently then cast his blue, squinty eyes on something cherished but breakable. Later I would hear the awful sound of that object smashing to the floor as he 'de-cluttered' the house!

When he was sent outside, which was often to say the least, he would become the ruthless destroyer of all living things, mostly rare birds. Not a good idea when one of you writes bird notes!!

He lived with us for 21 happy years – old in cat years – and as he aged he became contented and mellow and less destructive. We got him a warm companion to cuddle up to – a big, ginger moggy called Tarzan who I think had a calming influence on him mainly because Tarzan grew to be the biggest and Chang Chang had to concede to the new 'Boss'! - so much for the inscrutable Siamese.

PS. If you see a furniture van make sure your cat is safely indoors. No it never happened – but it nearly did. You know how inquisitive cats are?!!!

***

Barbara Jones

THE ROWNTREES REUNION

Well I went. I went and did it!! I went in a mixture of nerves and excitement up to York recently for the reunion, every 10 years, of the office staff at Rowntrees where I used to work before it was Rowntree MacIntosh and before finally being taken over by Nestles and re-locating to Croydon.

I worked at Rowntrees in York for 10 happy years before moving here 32 years ago. I'd returned 10 years ago for the previous reunion (the first one since my move here) and it was wonderful and everyone was instantly recognisable so why this time, 10 years later, did I hardly recognise anyone at all? Anno Domini I suppose!!

But this time, having been reunited with all those still here (quite a lot thankfully) and having talked, listened and observed it became clear that everyone was just the same underneath and hadn't changed much at all. A few more wrinkles and grey hairs but what the hell the important bond is still there and always will be and that's what matters and I'm so glad I went. We all enjoyed the camaraderie as we did when we all worked together.

Most of them, now retired, have the most interesting lives and grandchildren and exotic holidays were discussed not to mention all the good times in the old days and trips down memory lane. Those not yet retired have all found interesting jobs; no one has wasted their talents. In fact my friend Irene and her husband 'My 'arry' actually sold their house and went to work in Africa with famine stricken children. Very brave – I'd never have thought it of them - especially of 'My 'arry'. That's real guts.

Some have gone to live in Spain, others in Scotland and one lady visits the Galapogos Islands – to bird watch? Everyone was thrilled that I'd made the effort to go and were interested in what I'd been doing and one sweet lady asked if I still had my collection of wigs that I used to change every day. I didn't like to tell her that it was Felicity and not me! I never had a wig but as it made me sound more interesting than I was I didn't want to spoil her memories as she was certain it was me and Felicity had moved to Finland with her Finish husband years ago!

Meanwhile, Bernard and our friend Mary, who lives in Easingwold near York, after taking me to the venue, went for a meal in York and for a moment I almost bottled out and joined them but I'm so glad I didn't.

When they came to collect me everyone remembered Bernard and more memories were unleashed so we stayed even longer before retiring to a lovely hotel.

But the next day guess who was unleashed to explore all the wonderful sights and shops in York? No prizes for guessing. We shopped and explored having almost forgotten how lively and buzzing York is; the University students, tourists and street artists make it that way.

Since returning home there's been follow up news saying how good it was that I was there. So it was well worth going and its been decided that the next reunion will be in two years, not ten, so I'm now really looking forward to it.

***

Barbara Jones

THE STORY OF RAGGY LUGS' LUG

BY RAGGY LUGS – THE WORLD'S MOST HANDSOME RETRIEVER

Hello everyone, Woof! Woof! Since I last wrote which actually was the last time I've had a badly swollen left ear flap with a lot of loose blood inside which the Vet said was probably caused by me banging my ear rather heavily against something or shaking my head violently. I don't remember doing either of those things but that's not to say I didn't do it! But dogs like me who have large earflaps are very vulnerable to injury so we have to be careful of our floppy ears.

So the Vet had to anaesthetise me and operate on my ear to release the blood. I woke up feeling very groggy and my lovely ear flap was bereft of fur and covered in a tapestry of stitches making it feel very sore and, due to the missing fur, very cold too – to which Bernard added that I ought to have the added protection of, wait for it.....an ear wig!!! Oh how we laughed?!! He has to have his little joke...

Now fast forward if you will ten days and hurray its today and I've just had my stitches out and I feel much better and less itchy although I didn't ever scratch my ear – honestly really. The Vet said I'd been very brave but I'm glad it's all over.

But guess what? This morning when I woke my front left foot aches and when I try to walk I'm very stiff and hesitant. The Vet has given me medication and its worked so I'm very lucky. I guess its old age and poverty and there's nothing anyone can do about that!

***

Barbara's Quirky Tales

THE THOUGHTS AND WORKS OF RAGGY LUGS - OR BRADLEY IF YOU WOULD PREFER

Hello and woof to you all. Remember me? I'm Bradley and here I am again the world's most handsome retriever. Well that's what they say and who's to argue? SHE always wants to cuddle me, so suffocating. I'll politely offer my paw if you're lucky. After all one has to keep a sense of decorum and live up to what's expected of my pedigree. SHE says if I was slithery and covered in scales she wouldn't want to cuddle me so if by some miracle I changed into a python she'd leave me alone but then so would everyone else and I wouldn't like that and they'd get rid of me.

I've just celebrated my tenth birthday. Getting on a bit in dog years and I'm rather large with big feet but muscular rather than fat. Oh well perhaps a touch of fat. Maybe it's the beer!!

Barbara Jones

Now that I'm old would they really get rid of me? Makes me wonder can they still afford to keep me now I'm old. After all they're not exactly young either and my big bag of food that comes by post is shrinking as we speak. Are they economising 'cos this year they went to Devon instead of Provence where they sometimes go? But on the other hand they never used to take me abroad so maybe they were only thinking of my welfare when they took me to Devon. More of that later.

Hush! Was that the doorbell? Must bark and growl and look menacing. But no! Stop! My food has arrived. Oh joy, there is a god and it seems I am staying. I do puff a bit when we return from a long walk but I keep up and don't get lame or exhausted. SHE calls me a big choo choo puffer and says I'm the 7.45 to Charing Cross the one she used to catch. How silly. If I'm to be called a train then I insist on being called the Orient Express! At least that has some status. Or maybe the Euro Star. One can dream.

Perhaps I'm too sensitive because SHE fantasises about other dogs in front of me. Makes me feel insecure sometimes. The latest is about having three Westies called Mabel, Maud and Mildred. Imagine that, three females in one house all yapping at once. I couldn't stand that and I don't think my master could either. So it wouldn't happen.

Back to the holiday! It was gorgeous weather and it didn't rain so I didn't bring mud into the posh hotel. I did wonder if the carpet could be enhanced if a brown paw pattern was introduced but decided my expert artistry would not be appreciated. Everyone made a fuss of me and there were other dogs to chat to. We visited lots of nice places in north Devon but SHE got disorientated because the sea faced north something not experienced before and she said it looked dull with no sun sparkling on it. West coasts are her favourite. The shimmering sea and the quality of light are so uplifting, so magical. I think she's barmy! A good roll in the sand is what she needs. I certainly didn't care which way the sea faced; it was exhilarating to breathe sea air.

It was lovely to be in touch again. I'll write sometime soon. Right now must go and roll on the lawn.

***

Barbara Jones

THE THOUGHTS AND WORKS OF RAGGY LUGS
Part 2 - CHRISTMAS EDITION

Hello there, bet you didn't think I'd be back again so soon did you? Well neither did I but its all HER fault! Writer's block SHE calls it, how pretentious, so here I am to the rescue. Don't know what would happen without me. If she became a proper writer I'd certainly have my work cut out wouldn't I every time she got stuck? Would I get half the royalties for the first novel and film rights do you think? Perhaps I'll be cast in the leading role of 'Bradley Come Home'. Watch out Brad Pitt I'm on your tail so to speak – or is it my tail?! This is getting very silly so let's talk about the festive season from a dog's point of view.

This year at Scarborough we've also got a 70th birthday party and a wedding. Oh joy!! I love watching everyone getting dressed up in posh clothes but I'll be shut in the kitchen with my old mate Jake a white, fluffy Samoyed. Then at the last minute we'll push through the door and greet everyone affectionately rubbing round legs and jumping up in our loving way. We think the white and gold fur deposits on them will enhance dark suits and dresses. Pity no one else agrees – but oh, we will enjoy it! Perhaps we should ask Santa for clothes brushes for everyone. What do you think-generous or what?! Also to add to my laurels I'm an expert at knocking hats off. Guaranteed to break the ice at weddings if hats are worn of course – hope so!

On Christmas Eve we all sing carols in true tradition. We sing one about three wise men. SHE says she's never met one yet let alone three! We let her have her little joke. Same one every year – how boring!!

After they've all gone to bed Jake and I wait for Santa to come down the chimney arguing over which leg to grab when he does but he must come a different way 'cos we never see him. Always at this time Jake, being an Arctic dog, tells me how he used to help Rudolph to pull Santa's sleigh. I hasten to remind him it wasn't like that but he has his fantasies. I will not spoil them, its Christmas and we all have our dreams don't we?

Next day presents are exchanged and we buy each other doggy chocs and chews and toys. Then we fight over them! Well what else is there to do? He wants a new dog bowl with his name on it and I ask why?!! I mean surely no one else would want to eat from it so why the name? But he likes to be possessive.

Everyone pigs out at dinner, especially the humans, you'd think they'd never seen food before. Then, due to digestive exhaustion they fall asleep during the Queen's Speech. Jake and I watch for the Welsh Corgis but they rarely appear. Nasty things Corgis. Why doesn't she have decent dogs like Pyreneans or Labradoodles? I suppose its loyalty to the Welsh. Not only that but she never wears her crown. Why not? If you've got it flaunt it – that's what they are always telling me.

Then it's time for food again. Why? At least SHE doesn't over eat, says the sight of all that food puts her off. That's good; at least she doesn't have to lose all the extra weight afterwards.

Jake and I always discuss whether to capture the fairy from the top of the tree but know we'd be banned from the house if we did. They once had a cat who did that and caused so much damage it was exiled to the shed. Not worth it, we prefer to snooze by the fire. In the evening they sing silly songs and we join in. Woof, Woof. Gives the works of J.S.Bach a whole new meaning!! The rest of the time is spent on walkies by the sea, visiting friends and trekking the moors. SHE doesn't come. Her idea of the great outdoors is a day at Harrods!!

Time for goodbyes and home to a quiet New Year. Oh and happy that as well.

See you up the woods...

***

Barbara's Quirky Tales

TIGER, TIGER BURNING BRIGHT

Seeing a World Wildlife photo of a beautiful tiger in a magazine with the caption "What will you do when I've gone?" reduced me to tears because the truth hit me. Will our grandchildren ever know the pleasure of seeing these beautiful cats even if most of them are now in captivity. You'd have to be very lucky and extremely patient to see one in the wild these days. Just imagine going on safari to India or Africa and not seeing a tiger or lion at all. I would end up feeling very short changed.

So we go to safari parks where we know for certain we will see them all happily well fed and snoozing in the sun. We know that ideally they should be roaming wild in their native habitat but most of them have been hunted almost to extinction for their skins, bones used for potions and for sport. We see old photographs of upper class twits in the 1930's all posing in their pith helmets with the dead tigers they've just shot. Oh if only it could be the other way round! Tigers revenge on the upper classes. Now that I would like to see. Big cats, I hear, are now being bred for release into the wild. Thank goodness times have changed. We must preserve them.

When visiting Kent we love to go to Port Lympne Wild Animal Park on the Romney Marshes, to John Aspinall's Reserve also to be found at Howletts near Canterbury. His son has now taken over since his father sadly died. Port Lympne and Howletts have mostly Siberian tigers and other animals all living in excellent surroundings with lots of land. Also there is a big old house at Port Lympne on a hill overlooking the Romney Marshes and you can have afternoon tea. John Aspinall certainly put his money to good use with the Wild Animal Trust.

A few years ago at Port Lympne we saw a vision quite majestic to behold. There in a field sitting outside a large wooden shed, his home, was the biggest Siberian tiger I had ever seen, or so I thought, all muscles and thick, stripy fur, obviously the male. (The large bone structure and thick fur for coping in cold climates make them much bigger than Bengal tigers). Then the door was pushed open to reveal a huge mass of stripes totally filling the entrance and the stripes started coming out and coming out until everywhere was filled with stripes. Then the stripes stood up straight, stretched and yawned and I realized that this indeed was the male and the other his lady. He then shook himself, sniffed and started to nuzzle her whereupon she growled and pushed him away. I shouted, "Tell him you've got a headache!" He heard me and decided to investigate. Down he sauntered all muscles rippling to the small pond by the wire fence where we stood – on the other side obviously!! He took a drink, realized we were boring humans out of reach, turned tail and headed back to his lady hoping to have his wicked way, but she, sensing this, had wisely walked off!

Years later we saw them again, Darby and Joan still together sitting on the roof of their home only this time she appeared to be blind in one eye which looked like a white glass marble. Their keeper said it was a cataract and would be removed when ready but apart from that they were in fine form. I hope they still are. We need to save all endangered creatures. They are precious.

***

Barbara's Quirky Tales

THE TOURIST TRAP

Spring has, I think, finally arrived turning one's thoughts to days out or, if you're lucky, weekends in lovely places like the seaside, the Cotswolds, the Lake District or anywhere that's worth a visit.

Nothing's better than going with friends and spending the time browsing in gift shops followed by afternoon tea in quaint little olde worlde tea shops stuffing yourself silly on scones with lots of jam and cream. Very bad but oh so good!

Pretty though those places are the word twee comes to mind. All these senior citizens, myself included, spending the dosh in gift shops selling everything you've never wanted! I don't know why I, or anyone else, should want a linen tea towel with old churches printed on it or a teapot shaped like a rabbit but when everyone else is buying one you have to buy one too especially if it says 'a present from wherever'! I don't think so.

Seriously though I think there are some lovely luxury goods like exotic smelling toiletries, pretty jewellery, fabulous pottery and pictures etc. Very useful for buying presents. And books of course not to mention art galleries you can visit if you are rich. Oh and lots of sumptuous food. It always goes down well as presents.

But then, in the midst of all this you see a sign 'TO THE MODEL VILLAGE'. What's this all about? I mean here we are in the actual village so why on earth would we want to see a model of it! Is this for midgets do you think? I expect Americans would like it. You can imagine Doris and Wilber from Arkansas saying 'Aw gee folks we discovered this cute little place to have tea. It was called Fluid-on-the-Lung or something like that'. Well why not when you think about it. If you can have Bourton-on-the-Water then why not Fluid-on-the-Lung?

Barbara Jones

I've just remembered friends Pete and Anne who visited us in York years ago. We asked them if they wanted to see the sights. I'll never forget what Pete said. It was so funny and so true. He said 'Oh God now we've got to get back in the car when we've just got here and we have to say ' <u>Isn't</u> it pretty through here' and 'we <u>must</u> stop for afternoon tea' and 'Isn't this a quaint little eyesore – sorry village' – and 'we have to say 'isn't it lovely' and ' what a delightful old church' and 'we <u>do</u> have the scones and jam don't we?' and ' then we have to buy Auntie Mabel a pot plant from this vastly expensive gift shop' and 'Oh we <u>are</u> having fun <u>aren't we</u>' and 'we love nothing better than a traffic jam' and 'I'm <u>so</u> glad we came. We are so enjoying it and <u>so</u> glad we came' and 'can we queue for ice cream please?' He really epitomised what its all about.

Talking of York reminds me there used to be very talented real artisans making superb original works of art. Where are they now? These days there is nothing really worth buying only tacky stuff from the Far East.

I saw a cheap china model of Durham Cathedral in Stonegate, York of all places and I asked why it wasn't York Minster. I was told that tourists don't notice the difference. How sad but I don't believe it's true.

But maybe it is, I don't know.

***

WHAT A SCORCHER

We moved to Grinshill from York in 1976 and here we are 30 years later with another long, hot summer. We actually moved on 17th June 1976 and a week or so later the then Chairman of the Parish Council, Mr Frank Wycherley, called an urgent meeting in Grinshill Village Hall of representatives from Clive and Grinshill Parish Councils together with as many parishioners as possible. We decided, as newcomers, that we should attend and duly sat with a lot of people we didn't know in a packed village hall. Mr Wycherley explained that he had called the meeting because of the danger of fire on the hill and introduced the local Fire Chief to give us some advice. The Chief's main emphasis was to keep a lookout for smoke or flames and to call the fire service if necessary. He also advised that it would be useful if Clive and Grinshill could provide some volunteer 'Pickets' to patrol the hill and advise visitors not to smoke or light fires etc. He suggested that the people of Clive patrol to the top of Grinshill Hill and the Grinshill people patrol Corbet Wood.

There were mutters of approval, noddings of heads and general praise for a good, practical suggestion.

The Chief then asked if there were any questions. We heard one chap say that his 'man' would be a picket but the funniest was a dear old lady with a rather 'posh' voice who asked "What if there's a fire in the Corbet Wood which is seen by the Clive picket at the top of the hill but they don't tell anyone?" Of course we had to stifle our giggles but the Chief was very diplomatic and said, "Yes I see what you are saying, that is that the Clive people will think that the Grinshill people will have reported it. What I suggest is that anyone who sees a fire reports it to us immediately – we honestly don't mind how many calls we get so long as we get to know".

Great fun and a lovely introduction to what has become home.

***

WHITE WATER WOBBLE

Wobble was what we did, or, rather, what I did when we were invited to go on a white water canoe trip with some friends of Bernard's sister Liza when we stayed with her in Atlanta. That was after our tornado experience of which I wrote last time.

So it was with fear and trepidation that we approached the mighty Chattahoochee River. This river bears no resemblance at all to our gentle, peaceful, meandering River Severn as we realized when a huge log came tumbling and crashing its way downstream at great speed while being tossed high through boiling white foam.

As we stood on the bank, wearing inflatable jackets our new 'friends' Janet and Dennis gave us a short instruction on how to paddle these big Canadian canoes while kneeling upright on knee pads; how to 'draw' and 'crossdraw', how to avoid standing waves and the whirlpools and how to avoid the river edges which can pull you under and if this happens just bring your legs up and float till rescued, by whom I wondered as there didn't appear to be anyone else around! The edges, by the way, are home to various breeds of huge, poisonous snakes! Oh what joy - here we go!

Dennis led the way solo in his canoe followed by Bernard and Liza in theirs then, lastly, I followed in ours with Janet who was eight month's pregnant with the much wanted, long awaited child. Oh God please don't let me capsize us!

Thankfully Janet was in control so off we went. Dennis shouted 'If in doubt just keep paddling' so we did and built up a tremendous speed, only to see a six arch viaduct looming ahead where the rapids seemed at their worst. The canoe filled up, I prayed , and, somehow, we came out the other side without capsizing or colliding with the viaduct.

Barbara Jones

Then I saw an aircraft low in the sky and wished I was on it heading home !

However, the worst was over and we were starting to enjoy it but the Pizza House on the river bank signalled journey's end and was beckoning to us so we all enjoyed a good end to the day before driving back.

One thing's for certain, its impossible to paddle upstream so we just had to return in the comfort of the car which had been pre-parked ready for us. Oh thank God for that!

The Chattahoochee River was where they filmed 'Deliverance', a film about four young city men from Atlanta on an adventure weekend and we all know what happened to them don't we?..........Don't we???

***

Barbara's Quirky Tales

Z-A: LETTER TO THE GAS BOARD

Dear Sir,

Your fitter wanted to try it out in a cool place but I think it's better in the cupboard under the stairs. I must say I don't like it as much in the kitchen as I did in the shop window.

Since you put the new pipe from the mains into our house me and my husband dread going to bed because of the slight discharge; we think there is a leak just after it enters. I told my husband it was safe to leave it in all night but he won't. If he comes into the showroom like I did can the lady satisfy him behind the counter and talk him into it.

I have heard there are two you can have but it works out cheaper the more you get if you have it the other way. Oh, and I'm not satisfied with the apprentice so will you send a man to do it properly.

I shall try to pay you before the end of the month because my husband will be surprised if you cut it off without telling him. My husband is pretty handy but he says your men can do it better because of their tools.

Since I made an arrangement with your salesman I am having a baby and would like to change it for a drying cabinet. My husband was under the impression that I was getting it at a reduced rate but your salesman didn't use his head and got me into trouble.

Yours in expectation

***